Math Boosters

Problem Solving with Ratios & Proportions

To parents

This workbook is designed for children to complete by themselves. By checking their answers and correcting errors on their own, children can strengthen their independence and develop into self-motivated learners.

At Kumon, we believe that each child should do work according to their ability, rather than their age or grade level. So, if this workbook is too difficult or too easy for your child, please choose another Kumon Math Workbook with an appropriate level of difficulty.

How to use this book

1. **Let's get started!** Start by writing the date on the top of each page so you can track your progress.
2. **Let's go!** Start with Step 1 and review what you already know.
3. **Don't forget!** Read the "Don't Forget" boxes, which contain helpful explanations and examples.
4. **Let's work!** Solve the problems in numerical order, step-by-step. Look at the sample problems for help and return to the "Review" box if you need to refresh your knowledge.
5. **Let's check your answers!** After you have finished solving the problems, check your answers and add up your score on each page. If you don't know how to do this, ask your parent or guardian to show you.
6. **Let's get it right!** Once you have finished checking your answers, review any errors to see where you made a mistake and then try again.

Math Boosters Grades 4-6 Problem Solving with Ratios & Proportions

Table of Contents

Rounding

Rounding Large Numbers

Date / /

Score /100

Don't Forget!

- You can make numbers easier to work with by **rounding** them. Rounding is replacing some of the final digits of a number with zeroes. The rounded number is approximate—it is close to the original number, though not exactly the same.
- How to round to the thousands place:
  - If the number in the hundreds place is 0, 1, 2, 3, or 4, round it down to the nearest thousand.
  - If the number in the hundreds place is 5, 6, 7, 8, or 9, round it up to the nearest thousand.

1 **Round the following numbers to the nearest thousand.** 5 points per question

Example **To round numbers to the nearest thousand:**

2,350 (3 is in the hundreds place, so round down) ⇨ 2,000
2,650 (6 is in the hundreds place, so round up) ⇨ 3,000

(1) 2,513

(2) 7,365

(3) 3,675

(4) 4,823

(5) 50,360

(6) 62,734

(7) 63,851

(8) 99,964

Think about how you know when to round down or up.

2 Round the following numbers to the nearest ten thousand.

4 points per question

(1) 63,450

(2) 67,320

(3) 20,398

(4) 85,263

(5) 176,532

(6) 234,789

(7) 863,479

(8) 1,735,682

3 Round the following numbers to the nearest hundred thousand.

4 points per question

(1) 1,524,820

(2) 2,679,533

(3) 459,978

(4) 5,238,778

(5) 7,835,671

(6) 997,536

(7) 864,373

When rounding to the nearest **hundred thousand**, look at the digit in the **ten thousands** place.

Rounding
Estimating with Rounded Numbers

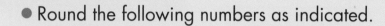

Review STEP 1

- Round the following numbers as indicated.

(1) Round 247,898 to the nearest ten thousand.

(2) Round 784,362 to the nearest hundred thousand.

1 **Estimate the answers. Use numbers rounded to the nearest hundred.**

8 points per question

Example To estimate the answer using numbers rounded to the nearest hundred:

$172 + 189$
⇩ ⇩
$200 + 200 = 400$

$335 - 246$
⇩ ⇩
$300 - 200 = 100$

(1) $357 + 126$

$400 + 100 =$ ⬚

(2) $576 - 273$

$600 - 300 =$ ⬚

(3) $2,087 + 326$

(4) $7,721 - 954$

(5) $285 + 349 + 1,768$

STEP 1-2
Rounding

STEP 3-6
Introduction to Ratios

STEP 7-15
Percentages

STEP 16-24
Unit Rates

STEP 25-40
Ratios and Proportions

STEP 41-47
Analyzing Data

STEP 48-53
Number of Possible Outcomes

2 Estimate the answers. Use numbers rounded to the nearest hundred.

7 points per question

(1) 620×391
$600 \times 400 =$

(2) $630 \div 242$
$600 \div 200 =$

(3) 514×295

(4) $39,290 \div 333$

(5) $384 \times 4,375$

(6) $4,025 \div 2,049$

3 You are planning to buy the following three items.

6 points per question

$463

$146

$280

(1) Which calculation is most useful for estimating how much money will you need?

(2) Which calculation shows exactly how much money you will need?

(3) Which calculation is most useful for determining whether $1,000 will be enough?

a $400 + 100 + 200$ *b* $463 + 146 + 280$ *c* $460 + 150 + 280$ *d* $500 + 200 + 300$

7

Multiplicative Comparisons

Review STEP **2**

● Estimate the answers. Use numbers rounded to the nearest hundred.

(1) 3,062 + 451

(2) 623 × 222

1 Answer the following questions.

10 points per question

Example How many times greater is 8 meters (m) compared to 4 meters?

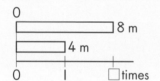

$8 \div 4 = 2$

⟨Ans.⟩ **2 times**

You can think of 4 meters as 1 unit. 8 meters would then be 2 of those units.

(1) How many times greater is 20 meters compared to 5 meters?

$$\boxed{} \div \boxed{} = \boxed{} \text{ times}$$

(2) How many times greater is 55 meters compared to 11 meters?

$$\boxed{55} \div \boxed{11} = \boxed{} \text{ times}$$

(3) How many times greater is 180 meters compared to 4 meters?

$$\boxed{} \div \boxed{} = \boxed{} \text{ times}$$

2 Answer the following questions.

10 points per question

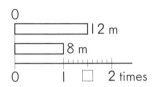

$12 \div 8 = 1.5$

You can think of 8 meters as 1 unit.

12 meters would then be 1.5 of those units.

(1) How many times greater is 50 centimeters compared to 20 centimeters?

☐ ÷ ☐ = ☐ times

(2) How many times greater is 30 grams compared to 20 grams?

☐ ÷ ☐ = ☐ times

(3) How many times greater is 46 kilometers compared to 20 kilometers?

☐ ÷ ☐ = ☐ times

(4) How many times greater is 130 kilograms compared to 50 kilograms?

☐ ÷ ☐ = ☐ times

(5) How many times greater is 2,800 milliliters compared to 800 milliliters?

☐ ÷ ☐ = ☐ times

(6) How many times greater is 1,800 liters compared to 1,500 liters?

☐ ÷ ☐ = ☐ times

(7) How many times greater is 11,250 dollars compared to 2,500 dollars?

☐ ÷ ☐ = ☐ times

All the answers on this page will be decimals.

Review STEP 3

● Answer the following questions.

(1) How many times greater is 30 meters compared to 10 meters?

☐ ÷ ☐ = ☐ times

(2) How many times greater is 5,400 grams compared to 1,200 grams?

☐ ÷ ☐ = ☐ times

1 Answer the following questions.

10 points per question

Example

The length of A is 6 meters (m).
A is twice the length of B.
What is the length of B?

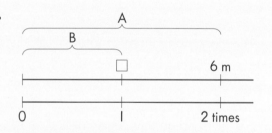

You can think of ☐ meters as 1 unit. 6 meters is 2 of those units.

So: ☐ × 2 = 6

⇩

6 ÷ 2 = 3   ⟨Ans.⟩   3 m

(1) The height of A is 12 meters. A is 2 times the height of B. What is the height of B?

12 ÷ 2 = ☐   ⟨Ans.⟩   m

(2) The height of A is 60 meters. A is 3 times the height of B. What is the height of B?

⟨Ans.⟩   m

2 Answer the following questions.

16 points per question

（1） The height of A is 12 meters. A is 1.5 times the height of B. What is the height of B?

$$12 \div 1.5 = 8$$

⟨Ans.⟩ _____ m

（2） The price of A is 2,800 dollars. A is 3.5 times the price of B. What is the price of B?

⟨Ans.⟩ _____ dollars

（3） The mass of A is 630 grams. A is 1.8 times the mass of B. What is the mass of B?

⟨Ans.⟩ _____ g

（4） The area of A is 13.8 square kilometers. A is 0.6 times the area of B. What is the area of B?

⟨Ans.⟩ _____ km²

（5） The mass of A is 124.5 kilograms. A is 0.15 times the mass of B. What is the mass of B?

⟨Ans.⟩ _____ kg

Review STEP 4

- The mass of A is 12.5 grams. A is 0.5 times the mass of B. What is the mass of B?

⟨Ans.⟩ _____ g

1 **Anna (A), Bess (B), and Cary (C) played in a basketball game. The table shows the number of goals each person scored and the total number they attempted.** 10 points per question

Goals in the Basketball Game	A	B	C
Goals scored	6	14	3
Total attempted	10	20	15

(1) Look at the column with Anna's data. How many times as many is the number of goals scored compared to the total number attempted?

goals   total

$\boxed{6} \div \boxed{10} = \boxed{}$

⟨Ans.⟩ _____ times

(2) For Bess, how many times as many is the number of goals scored compared to the total number attempted?

⟨Ans.⟩ _____ times

(3) For Cary, how many times as many is the number of goals scored compared to the total number attempted?

⟨Ans.⟩ _____ times

Don't Forget!

- A **ratio** can be expressed as a comparison of two values using division. A ratio shows how large or small one value is in comparison to another.

$$\boxed{\text{ratio} = \text{value 1} \div \text{value 2}}$$

- Sometimes when we are comparing two values, one of them is a standard or base value that we want to compare the other value to. (Often, the base value is the total value or the total number of times that something happens.) Set up these ratios like this:

$$\boxed{\text{ratio} = \text{compared value} \div \text{base value}}$$

- You can indicate a ratio in different ways—for example, using a decimal, a percentage, a fraction, or ratio notation (with a colon).

2 Answer the questions below. Write each ratio as a decimal or whole number.

14 points per question

(1) Suppose you correctly answered 7 out of 10 questions. What is the ratio of the number of questions you answered correctly to the total number of questions?

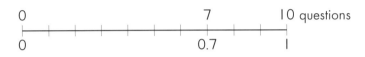

ratio in
decimal form

⟨Ans.⟩ _____

(2) Suppose you won 3 out of 5 basketball games. What is the ratio of the number of games you won to the total number of games you played?

☐ ÷ ☐ = ☐

⟨Ans.⟩ _____

(3) Suppose you lost 2 out of 5 basketball games. What is the ratio of the number of games you lost to the total number of games you played?

☐ ÷ ☐ = ☐

⟨Ans.⟩ _____

(4) Suppose you won 7 out of 7 soccer games. What is the ratio of the number of games you won to the total number of games you played?

7 ÷ 7 = ☐

⟨Ans.⟩ _____

(5) Suppose you made 5 guesses and they were all incorrect. What is the ratio of the number of correct guesses to the total number of guesses you made? (Consider the total number as the base value you are comparing to.)

0 ÷ 5 = ☐

⟨Ans.⟩ _____

Comparing Ratios in Decimal Form

Review STEP 5

● Suppose you correctly answered 8 out of 10 questions. What is the ratio of the number of questions you answered correctly to the total number of questions? Write the answer as a decimal.

⟨Ans.⟩ _____

1 Find the ratio of the number of boys to the total number of children. Then find the ratio of the number of girls to the total number of children. Write the value of each ratio as a decimal.

9 points per question

(1)

7 boys and 3 girls

Ratio of boys to total: $7 \div 10 =$

Ratio of girls to total:

(2)

1 boy and 3 girls

Ratio of boys to total:

Ratio of girls to total:

(3)

6 boys and 9 girls

Ratio of boys to total:

Ratio of girls to total:

For these problems, set up the ratio this way: ratio = compared value ÷ base value

2 The area of a gym is 800 square meters (m²) and the area of a volleyball court is 128 m². Compare the area of the volleyball court to the area of the gym. (Consider the area of the gym as the base value you are comparing to.) Write your answer as a decimal.

10 points

compared value   base value   ratio

$$128 \div \boxed{} = \boxed{}$$

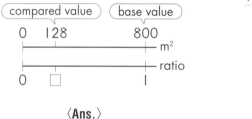

〈Ans.〉 _____

3 Elliot has a strip of ribbon as shown below. Compare each length of the ribbon, A and B, to the ribbon's total length. Write your answers as decimals.

9 points per question

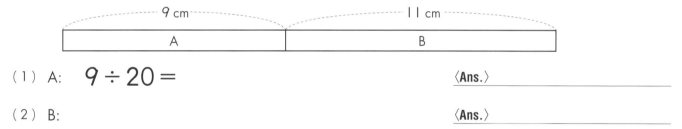

(1) A: $9 \div 20 =$ 〈Ans.〉 _____

(2) B: 〈Ans.〉 _____

4 Three school clubs—soccer, tennis, and music—held tryouts. The table shows the number of people allowed in each club and the number that tried out.

9 points per question

Club	Number allowed	How many tried out
Soccer	30	24
Tennis	20	35
Music	15	12

(1) Find the ratio of the number of people who tried out for soccer to the number allowed in the club. Write your answer as a decimal.

$$24 \div 30 = \boxed{}$$

〈Ans.〉 _____

(2) Find the ratio of the number of people who tried out for tennis to the number allowed in the club. Write your answer as a decimal.

〈Ans.〉 _____

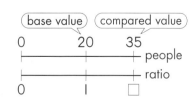

The value of a ratio can be greater than 1.

Introduction to Ratios as Percentages

Review STEP 6

● 30 people can join the tennis club. 18 people tried out for it. Find the ratio of the number of people who tried out to the number allowed. Write your answer as a decimal.

18 ÷ ☐ = ☐   ⟨Ans.⟩ _____

Don't Forget!   Percentage

You have seen that a ratio can be written as a decimal. Similarly, a ratio can be written as a percentage. In a **percentage**, the base value of the ratio is 100. The term "percent" (or the % symbol) tells you that a quantity is being compared to a base value of 100.

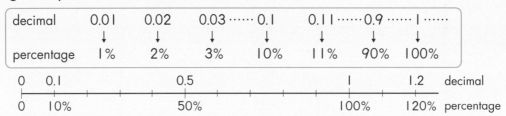

decimal	0.01	0.02	0.03 ······ 0.1	0.11 ······ 0.9 ······ 1 ······
	↓	↓	↓ ↓	↓ ↓ ↓
percentage	1%	2%	3% 10%	11% 90% 100%

You can convert a decimal to a percentage by multiplying by 100.

$$0.01 \times 100 = 1\%$$

1   Rewrite each decimal or whole number as a percentage.   3 points per question

(1) 0.04   ☐   (2) 0.16   ☐

(3) 0.09   ☐   (4) 0.45   ☐

(5) 0.4   ☐   (6) 1   ☐

(7) 1.08   ☐   (8) 2   ☐

(9) 0.005   ☐   (10) 0.806   ☐

2 Rewrite each percentage as a decimal or whole number.

4 points per question

(1) 3%   0.03

(2) 7%

(3) 14%

(4) 60%

(5) 98%

(6) 100%

(7) 250%

(8) 307%

(9) 0.8%

(10) 50.2%

3 Answer the questions below. Write each ratio as a percentage.

10 points per question

(1) Suppose you attempted 10 shots in a basketball game. You made 7 goals. What is the ratio of the number of goals to the total number of shots?

7 ÷ 10 =

⟨Ans.⟩ _____ %

(2) Suppose you attempted 25 shots in a basketball game. You made 15 goals. What is the ratio of the number of goals to the total number of shots?

⟨Ans.⟩ _____

(3) Suppose you had a 30-centimeter elastic band, and you stretched it to 42 centimeters. What is the ratio of the length of the stretched-out band, compared to its original length? (Consider the original length as the base value.)

⟨Ans.⟩ _____

Percentages in Context

Review STEP 7

● Rewrite the following decimals as percentages.

(1) 0.29

(2) 0.6

1 Answer the following questions.

10 points per question

Example The price of an item was 100 dollars. Now the item is on sale for 75 dollars. What percentage of the original price is the sale price?

compared value   base value   ratio

$75 \div 100 = 0.75$

⟨Ans.⟩ **75%**

(1) 100 grams of milk contains 3 grams of protein. What percentage of the milk is protein?

compared value   base value   ratio

$\boxed{3} \div \boxed{100} = \boxed{}$

⟨Ans.⟩

Ratio as a decimal × 100 = percentage (%)

(2) 150 milliliters of orange juice contains 120 milliliters of water. What percentage of the juice is water?

$\boxed{120} \div \boxed{} = \boxed{}$

⟨Ans.⟩

2 The price of an item was 650 dollars. Now the item is on sale for 520 dollars. What percentage of the original price is the sale price?

20 points

⟨Ans.⟩

3 The price of a bike was 400 dollars. Now the bike is on sale for 50 dollars less than the original price. By what percentage has the price decreased?

20 points

⟨Ans.⟩

4 The price of a plane ticket was 2,400 dollars. Now it has increased by 360 dollars. By what percentage has the price increased?

20 points

⟨Ans.⟩

5 Last year the population of the town was 6,420. This year the population decreased by 321. By what percentage did the population decrease?

20 points

⟨Ans.⟩

STEP **9**

Percentages

Finding a Percentage of a Whole

Date   /   /

Score

/100

Review STEP **8**

• The regular price of a suitcase was 200 dollars. Now the suitcase is on sale for 160 dollars. What percentage of the original price is the sale price?

⟨Ans.⟩ _____

1 Answer the following questions.

15 points per question

Example 35 people went to the dentist one day. 20% of them had cavities. Of the 35 people, how many had cavities?

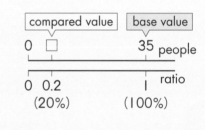

base value   ratio   compared value

$35 \times 0.2 = 7$

| base value | × | ratio | = | compared value |

⟨Ans.⟩   **7 people**

(1) A store had 500 notebooks. It sold 20% of them. How many notebooks did the store sell?

20% of 500 notebooks means 500 times 0.2 .

$500 \times \boxed{0.2} = \boxed{}$

⟨Ans.⟩ _____

(2) A bus can seat 75 people. There was a mix-up at the bus station, and more tickets were sold than there were seats. The number of tickets sold was 120% the number of seats. How many tickets were sold?

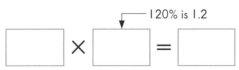

120% is 1.2

$\boxed{} \times \boxed{} = \boxed{}$

⟨Ans.⟩ _____

2 Answer the following questions.

10 points per question

(1) 30% of 100 grams is how many grams?

⟨Ans.⟩ _____

(2) 30% of 150 milliliters is how many milliliters?

⟨Ans.⟩ _____

(3) 85% of 700 dollars is how many dollars?

⟨Ans.⟩ _____

(4) 25% of 48 people is how many people?

⟨Ans.⟩ _____

(5) 150% of 300 people is how many people?

⟨Ans.⟩ _____

3 An apple is 85% water. How many grams of water are in a 320-gram apple?

20 points

⟨Ans.⟩ _____

21

Review STEP **9**

- A theater has 120 seats. There are people sitting in 70% of the seats. How many people are seated in the theater (assuming one person per seat)?

⟨Ans.⟩ _____

Don't Forget!

- A **discount** is a way to describe how a price has decreased.
- If the discount on the original price of an item is 30%, the item is sold for 30% less than the original price. A discount of 30% is the same as a sale price of 70%.

total percentage		discount percentage		sale percentage

$$100\% - 30\% = 70\%$$

- To calculate a price based on discount percentage, here is one method you can use:

  1. Use the discount percentage to find the sale percentage.
  2. Multiply the original price by the sale percentage.

1 **Answer the following questions.**   30 points

Example   Theo bought a 60-dollar item at a 30% discount. How much did he pay?

$1 - 0.3 = 0.7$ $60 \times 0.7 = 42$ ⟨Ans.⟩   42 dollars

Kelsey bought a 500-dollar item at a 25% discount. How much did she pay?

$1 - \boxed{0.25} = \boxed{}$ $500 \times \boxed{} = \boxed{}$

⟨Ans.⟩ _____

STEP 1-2
Rounding

STEP 3-6
Introduction to Ratios

STEP 7-15
Percentages

STEP 16-24
Unit Rates

STEP 25-40
Ratios and Proportions

STEP 41-47
Analyzing Data

STEP 48-53
Number of Possible Outcomes

2 When 5% sales tax is added to an item that costs 800 dollars, how much do you have to pay in all?   30 points

$$1 + \boxed{0.05} = \boxed{}$$

$$800 \times \boxed{} = \boxed{}$$

⟨Ans.⟩ _____

3 Last year in John's orange grove, John harvested 1,500 kilograms of oranges. This year, he harvested 20% more oranges than last year. How many kilograms of oranges did he harvest this year?   20 points

⟨Ans.⟩ _____

4 The number of students in an elementary school next year will be 6% fewer than this year. The number of students this year is 450. How many students will there be next year?   20 points

⟨Ans.⟩ _____

23

Percentages
Percentage Decrease and Increase, Method 2

Date / /

Score /100

Review STEP 10

● Elena bought a 700-dollar item at a 15% discount. How much did she pay?

⟨Ans.⟩ _____

Don't Forget!

Here is another way to calculate a price based on discount percentage:

1. Use the discount percentage to find how much money will be taken off.
2. Subtract that amount from the original price.

1 Answer the following question.

30 points

Example

Theo bought a 60-dollar item at a 30% discount. How much did he pay?

$60 \times 0.3 = 18$

$60 - 18 = 42$

⟨Ans.⟩ 42 dollars

Abby bought a 400-dollar item at a 25% discount. How much did she pay?

$400 \times \boxed{0.25} = \boxed{}$

$400 - \boxed{} = \boxed{}$

⟨Ans.⟩ _____

2 When 5% sales tax is added to an item that costs **200 dollars,** how much do you have to pay in all?   30 points

$$200 \times \boxed{0.05} = \boxed{}$$

$$200 + \boxed{} = \boxed{}$$

⟨Ans.⟩ _____

3 Last year in Ella's apple grove, Ella harvested **2,800 kilograms** of apples. This year, she harvested **30% more** apples than last year. How many kilograms of apples did she harvest this year?   20 points

$$\boxed{} \times \boxed{} = \boxed{}$$

⟨Ans.⟩ _____

4 The number of students in an elementary school next year will be **8% fewer** than this year. The number of students this year is **550.** How many students will there be next year?   20 points

$$\boxed{} \times \boxed{} = \boxed{}$$

⟨Ans.⟩ _____

25

Review STEP 11

● When 8% sales tax is added to an item that costs 300 dollars, how much do you have to pay in all?

☐ × ☐ =

⟨Ans.⟩ _____

---

1 **Answer the following question.**　　　　　　　20 points

Example

Your favorite snack food is now sold in packages of 120 grams (g). This is 20% more than the packages contained before. How many grams was a package of snacks before the increase?

$$120 ÷ 1.2 = 100$$
_{compared value}　_{ratio}　_{base value}

| compared value | ÷ | ratio | = | base value |

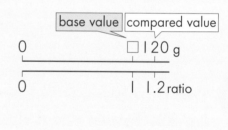

⟨Ans.⟩　　100 g

Malik's favorite snack food is now sold in packages of 156 grams. This is 30% more than the packages contained before. How many grams was a package of snacks before the increase?

⟨Ans.⟩ _____

2 90 tickets were sold for the bus. This is 20% more than the number of seats on the bus. How many seats are on the bus?

20 points

⟨Ans.⟩ _____

3 Tyler is growing flowers in a greenhouse. The area used for growing tulips is 84 square meters. This is 35% of the total area of the greenhouse. What is the total area of the greenhouse?

20 points

⟨Ans.⟩ _____

4 Maya bought a new computer at a 20% discount. She paid 560 dollars. What was the original price of the computer?

20 points

$$\boxed{} \div \boxed{0.8} = \boxed{}$$

⟨Ans.⟩ _____

5 A store sold 230 donuts today. This was 8% less than the number sold yesterday. How many donuts were sold yesterday?

20 points

⟨Ans.⟩ _____

STEP 13

Percentages

Band Charts and Pie Charts

Date   /   /

Score

/100

Review STEP 12

- Leo bought a train ticket at 20% off the regular price, and it was 120 dollars. What was the regular price?

⟨Ans.⟩

Don't Forget!   Band Charts and Pie Charts

- In a **band chart**, like the one shown below, a horizontal bar represents a total amount. The bar is divided up to show how much of the total amount comes from different categories.

| A | B | C | D | Other |

0   10   20   30   40   50   60   70   80   90   100%

  A is 50% of the total.   B is 20% of the total.
  C is 10% of the total.   D is 9% of the total.
  Other is 11% of the total.

- A **pie chart** is like a band chart, but the total is represented by a circle instead of a bar.

1 **The band chart shows data about the different types of crops grown in an area.**

8 points per question

Crops Grown

| Rice | Vegetables | Wheat | Other |

0   10   20   30   40   50   60   70   80   90   100%

(1) What percentage of the total crop production is rice?

⟨Ans.⟩   65 %

(2) What percentage of the total crop production is vegetables?

⟨Ans.⟩

(3) What percentage of the total crop production is wheat?

⟨Ans.⟩

STEP 1-2
Rounding

STEP 3-6
Introduction to Ratios

STEP 7-15
Percentages

STEP 16-24
Unit Rates

STEP 25-40
Ratios and Proportions

STEP 41-47
Analyzing Data

STEP 48-53
Number of Possible Outcomes

2 The band chart shows data about colors of cars in a city.

9 points per question

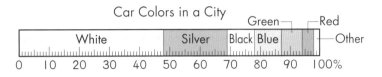

Car Colors in a City

(1) What percentage of the cars are white?

⟨Ans.⟩ _____

(2) What percentage of the cars are silver?

⟨Ans.⟩ _____

(3) About what portion of the cars are either blue or black? Write your answer as a fraction.

⟨Ans.⟩ about _____

(4) How many times as many silver cars are there compared to green cars?

⟨Ans.⟩ _____

3 The pie chart shows data about land use in a town.

10 points per question

(1) What percentage of the total land is residential?

⟨Ans.⟩ _____

(2) What percentage of the total land is farmland?

⟨Ans.⟩ _____

(3) About what portion of the total land is either roads or industrial area? Write your answer as a fraction.

⟨Ans.⟩ about _____

(4) About how many times as much farmland is there compared to industrial area?

⟨Ans.⟩ about _____

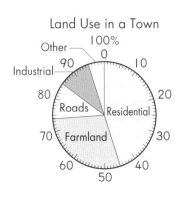

Land Use in a Town

Preparing Data for Pie Charts

Review STEP 13

• The pie chart on the right shows data about the kinds of domestic animals in a town.

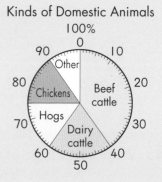

Kinds of Domestic Animals

(1) What percentage of the total domestic animals are dairy cattle?

⟨Ans.⟩ _____

(2) What portion of animals are either dairy cattle or chickens? Write your answer as a fraction.

⟨Ans.⟩ about _____

---

1 **The table on the right shows the number of elementary school students in four regions.**

(1) 10 points for complete, (2) 5 points, (3) 5 points per ☐

(1) Find the percentage of students living in each region. Write the appropriate numbers in the following equations.

students ÷ total students × 100 = percentage (100%)

East: $18 ÷ 40 × 100 = 45$ (%)

West: $12 ÷ 40 × 100 = $ (%)

North: $ ÷ × 100 = $ (%)

South: $ ÷ × 100 = $ (%)

Student Population by Region		
Region	Students	Percentage (%)
East	18	45
West	12	
North	6	
South	4	
Total	40	

(2) What is the sum of the percentages of each of these regions?

⟨Ans.⟩ _____ %

(3) Fill out the table by writing in the percentages.

2 The table on the right shows the number of injuries that occurred at different locations at school during one year.

(1) 9 points for complete, (2)(3) 8 points, (4) 8 points per ☐

(1) Find the percentage of injuries that occurred in each location. Write the appropriate numbers in the following equations. (Round decimals to the nearest ones place.)

Playground: ☐ ÷ ☐ × 100 = ☐ (%)

Gym: ☐ ÷ ☐ × 100 = ☐ (%)

Hallway: ☐ ÷ ☐ × 100 = ☐ (%)

Classroom: ☐ ÷ ☐ × 100 = ☐ (%)

Injuries by Location		
Location	Number of injuries	Percentage (%)
Playground	18	☐
Gym	15	☐
Hallway	4	☐
Classroom	3	☐
Total	40	☐

(2) What is the sum of the percentages in (1)?

⟨Ans.⟩ _____

Don't Forget!

The sum of the percentages may not add up to exactly 100% due to rounding. In some cases you may be asked to make adjustments so the total is exactly 100%. Do this by adding or subtracting 1% from the largest of the calculated percentages or from "other."

(3) In order to make the total percentage 100%, what could you change, according to the tip stated above?

⟨Ans.⟩ The percentage for ☐ could be ☐ %.

(4) Complete the table by writing in the percentages.

Remember rounding. 0, 1, 2, 3, or 4, round it down. 5, 6, 7, 8, or 9, round it up.

31

Percentages
Creating Pie Charts

Date   /   /
Score   /100

Review STEP 14

- For the table on the right, find the percentage of orders for each kind of drink so that the total is 100%, and fill out the table.

Number of Drinks Ordered		
Drink	Number of orders	Percentage (%)
Coffee	29	
Tea	21	26
Juice	17	
Water	13	16
Total	80	100

1 Complete the pie chart to show the percentages of each item in the table.

30 points

Example

To complete the pie chart based on the table, draw in a section of the "pie" for each percentage in the table. Use the numbers around the edge of the chart to see how large each section should be.

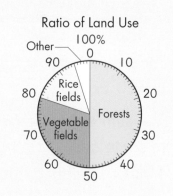

Ratio of Land Use

Ratio of Land Use					
Type	Forests	Vegetable fields	Rice fields	Other	Total
Percentage (%)	50	30	15	5	100

Number of Cans Collected					
Place	Road	Park	Riverside	Beach	Campsite	Total
Percentage (%)	56	14	13	12	5	100

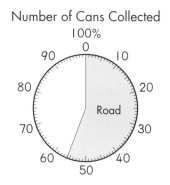

Number of Cans Collected

2 The table on the right shows data about the types of books in the class library.

(1)4 points per ☐ , (2)10 points

(1) Calculate the percentage for each type and fill out the table. (Round decimals to the nearest ones place. Make sure the percentages total to 100%.)

(2) Represent the table as a pie chart.

Types of Books in the Library
100%

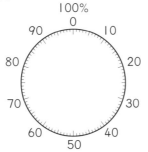

Types of Books in the Library		
Type	Books	Percentage (%)
Fiction	46	
Science	36	
History	26	
Other	12	
Total	120	

3 The table on the right shows data about the types of stores in a town.

(1)5 points per ☐ , (2)10 points

(1) Calculate the percentage for each type and fill out the table. (Round decimals to the nearest ones place. Make sure the percentages total to 100%.)

(2) Represent the table as a pie chart.

Types of Stores
100%

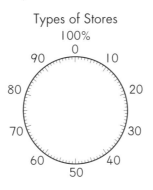

Types of Stores		
Type	Stores	Percentage (%)
Supermarket	29	
Electronics store	22	
Clothing store	17	
Flower store	3	
Other	19	
Total	90	

Rounding and Percentages

Review STEP 1   **Answer the following questions about rounding.**

5 points per ☐

(1) When rounding to the nearest ten, what is the lowest number that rounds to 80? What is the highest number that rounds to 80?

⟨Ans.⟩ ☐ , ☐

(2) When rounding to the nearest ten, what is the lowest number that rounds to 350? What is the highest number that rounds to 350?

⟨Ans.⟩ ☐ , ☐

Review STEP 2   **Estimate the answers. Use numbers rounded to the nearest hundred.**

5 points per question

(1) 294 + 145

⟨Ans.⟩ _____

(2) 8,422 − 1,674

⟨Ans.⟩ _____

(3) 513 × 285

⟨Ans.⟩ _____

(4) 4,625 ÷ 246

⟨Ans.⟩ _____

Review STEP 3 STEP 4   **Answer the following questions.**

5 points per question

(1) The height of building A is 30 meters. It is 1.5 times the height of building B. What is the height of building B?

⟨Ans.⟩   m

(2) The area of farm A is 27.6 square kilometers. It is 0.6 times the area of farm B. What is the area of farm B?

⟨Ans.⟩   km²

Review **STEP 5** **STEP 6** The 6th grade has 50 students, but 5 students are absent today. Find the ratio of the number of absent students to the total number in the grade. Write your answer as a decimal. 10 points

⟨Ans.⟩ _____

Review **STEP 7** **STEP 8** Rewrite the following decimals as percentages. 5 points per question

(1) 0.04

(2) 0.006

⟨Ans.⟩ _____

⟨Ans.⟩ _____

Review **STEP 9** – **STEP 12** A bus can seat 75 people. There was a mix-up at the bus station, and more tickets were sold than there were seats. The number of tickets sold was 140% the number of seats. How many tickets were sold? 10 points

⟨Ans.⟩ _____

Review **STEP 13** – **STEP 15** The pie chart on the right shows data about where 200 injuries occurred at school during the first semester. 10 points per question

(1) What percentage of injuries occurred on the playground?

⟨Ans.⟩ _____

(2) How many times as many injuries occurred in the classroom compared to the number of injuries in the hallway?
Write your answer as a fraction.

⟨Ans.⟩ _____

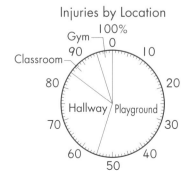

Injuries by Location

STEP **16**

Unit Rates
· ·

Introduction to Unit Rates

Date   /   /

Score

/100

Review STEP 15

- Complete the pie chart to show the data in the table below.

Percentages of Total Industrial Output			
Iron	Chemical	Textile	Other
55%	20%	17%	8%

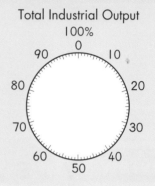

Total Industrial Output

Don't Forget!

- A **unit rate** is a ratio that relates one quantity to 1 unit of another quantity.
- For example, suppose you are in a crowded gymnasium. How could you describe how crowded it is? You could say how many people there are for every 1 square meter in the gym. Or, you could do the opposite: You could say how many square meters there are for every 1 person in the gym. Both of those comparisons are unit rates.

---

1 **The table on the right shows data about chicken coops A and B.**

(1)8 points, (2)10 points per question

(1) Which chicken coop is more crowded?

⟨**Ans.**⟩ _____

(2) Find the number of chickens per 1 square meter (m²) in each chicken coop.

Chicken coop A

8 ÷ 4 =

Chicken coop B

Chicken Coops A and B		
	Total area of coop (m²)	Number of chickens
A	4	8
B	4	10

⟨**Ans.**⟩ _____

⟨**Ans.**⟩ _____

2 The table on the right shows data about four rabbit hutches: A, B, C, and D.

8 points per question

(1) Which hutch is more crowded, A or B?

⟨Ans.⟩ _____

(2) Which hutch is more crowded, B or C?

⟨Ans.⟩ _____

Rabbit Hutches A, B, C, and D		
	Total area of hutch (m²)	Number of rabbits
A	6	9
B	6	8
C	5	8
D	9	15

(3) Find the number of rabbits per 1 square meter in each of the hutches listed below. (For decimal answers, round to the nearest tenth if needed.)

Rabbit hutch A

⟨Ans.⟩ _____

Rabbit hutch C

⟨Ans.⟩ _____

Rabbit hutch D

⟨Ans.⟩ _____

(4) Which is more crowded: a hutch that has more rabbits per 1 square meter or a hutch that has fewer rabbits per 1 square meter?

⟨Ans.⟩ _____

(5) Which hutch is most crowded: A, C, or D?

⟨Ans.⟩ _____

(6) Find the area per rabbit for each of the hutches below. (For decimal answers, round to the nearest hundredth if needed.)

Rabbit hutch A

⟨Ans.⟩ _____

Rabbit hutch C

⟨Ans.⟩ _____

Unit Rates

Population Density: An Example of a Unit Rate

Date / /

Score /100

Review STEP 16

- The table shows data about two swimming pools, A and B. Which pool is more crowded?

〈Ans.〉 _____

Community Swimming Pools		
	Area (m²)	Current number of swimmers
Pool A	540	40
Pool B	450	36

Don't Forget!

- **Population density** is a unit rate defined as the number of people per 1 unit of land area.

  population density = number of people ÷ land area

- Population density is a useful way to compare the number of people who live in different areas — you can use it to describe how "crowded" or "not crowded" a region is.

1 The table on the right shows data about two cities, A and B.

10 points per question

(1) Find the population density (people per 1 km²) of each city. Round answers to the nearest whole number.

Two Cities		
	Area (km²)	Population
City A	7,406	1,810,000
City B	5,678	1,440,000

City A

$1{,}810{,}000 \div 7{,}406 = 244.3\ldots$

〈Ans.〉 _____ people/km²

City B

☐ ÷ ☐ =

〈Ans.〉 _____ people/km²

(2) Which city has a higher population density?

〈Ans.〉 _____

2 **The table on the right shows data about three cities: A, B, and C.**

14 points per question

(1) Find the population density (people per 1 km²) of each city. Round answers to the nearest whole number.

Three Cities		
	Area (km²)	Population
City A	7,286	2,340,000
City B	3,691	1,400,000
City C	2,440	850,000

City A

$$2{,}340{,}000 \div 7{,}286 = 321.1\ldots$$

⟨Ans.⟩ _____

City B

$$\boxed{} \div \boxed{} =$$

⟨Ans.⟩ _____

City C

$$\boxed{} \div \boxed{} =$$

⟨Ans.⟩ _____

(2) Which city has the highest population density?

⟨Ans.⟩ _____

(3) Which city has the lowest population density?

⟨Ans.⟩ _____

Comparing Unit Rates

Date / /

Score /100

Review STEP **17**

- Town A has an area of 20 km² and a population of 7,400. Find the population density of this town.

⟨Ans.⟩ _____ **people/km²**

1 Answer the following questions.

17 points per question

Example

The table on the right shows data about the harvest from two potato fields, **A** and **B**. Find the mass of the potatoes per 1 square meter (m²).

Field A

$30 \div 12 = 2.5$ ⟨Ans.⟩ 2.5 kg/m²

Field B

$42 \div 15 = 2.8$ ⟨Ans.⟩ 2.8 kg/m²

Harvest from Two Potato Fields		
	Area (km²)	Kilograms (kg) harvested
Field A	12	30
Field B	15	42

(1) The table on the right shows data about the harvest from two potato fields, A and B. Find the mass of the potatoes per square meter (m²).

Harvest from Two Potato Fields		
	Area (m²)	Kilograms (kg) harvested
Field A	15	90
Field B	20	124

Field A

$\boxed{90} \div \boxed{15} = \boxed{}$

⟨Ans.⟩ _____

Field B

$\boxed{} \div \boxed{} = \boxed{}$

⟨Ans.⟩ _____

(2) Which field produced more per square meter?

⟨Ans.⟩ _____

2 Which is more expensive per book: 91 dollars for 7 books, or 72 dollars for 6 books?

<u>16 points</u>

91 dollars for 7 books

72 dollars for 6 books

⟨Ans.⟩ _____

3 Car A can travel 108 kilometers on 12 liters of gas. Car B can travel 152 kilometers on 16 liters of gas. Which car is more fuel efficient? (In other words, which car can go farther per liter?)

<u>16 points</u>

Car A

Car B

⟨Ans.⟩ _____

4 Rod A has a mass of 240 grams and is 3 meters long. Rod B has a mass of 370 grams and is 5 meters long. Which rod has more mass per meter?

<u>17 points</u>

Rod A

Rod B

⟨Ans.⟩ _____

Review STEP 18

• Yellow tape costs 20 dollars for 8 meters. White tape costs 13 dollars for 5 meters. Which tape is cheaper per meter?

Yellow tape

White tape

⟨Ans.⟩ _____

1 **Answer the following questions.**

13 points per question

Example

Metal wire costs 4 dollars per meter. How much does 12 meters of wire cost?

$4 \times 12 = 48$

⟨Ans.⟩ 48 dollars

How much wire can you buy with 90 dollars?

$90 \div 4 = 22.5$

⟨Ans.⟩ 22.5 m

(1) A car can travel 15 kilometers on 1 liter of gas. How many kilometers can the car travel on 32 liters of gas?

$\boxed{15} \times \boxed{} = \boxed{}$

⟨Ans.⟩ _____

(2) How many liters of gas does the car need to travel 630 kilometers?

$630 \div 15 =$

⟨Ans.⟩ _____

2 A gardener uses 0.5 kilograms of fertilizer for every 1 square meter of her garden.

13 points per question

(1) How many kilograms of fertilizer does she need for 8.4 square meters of garden?

⟨Ans.⟩ _____

(2) Over how many square meters can she spread 1.6 kilograms of fertilizer?

⟨Ans.⟩ _____

3 Printing machine A can print 450 sheets of paper in 5 minutes. Printing machine B can print 480 sheets of paper in 6 minutes.

12 points per question

(1) How many sheets of paper can each machine print per minute?

Machine A

⟨Ans.⟩ _____

Machine B

⟨Ans.⟩ _____

(2) How many sheets of paper can machine A print in 7 minutes?

⟨Ans.⟩ _____

(3) How many minutes does machine B take to print 1,200 sheets of paper?

⟨Ans.⟩ _____

Unit Rates
Introduction to Speed

Date / /

Score /100

Review STEP 19

- Pump A can pump 450 liters of water in 15 minutes. Pump B can pump 720 liters of water in 25 minutes. Which one can pump more water per minute?

⟨Ans.⟩ _____

Don't Forget!

- Speed can be found using the following formula.

$$ \text{distance} \div \text{time} = \text{speed} $$

(This formula gives the average speed during the time period.)
- Commonly used units of speed include kilometers per hour (km/h), meters per minute (m/min), and meters per second (m/s).

1 Answer the following questions.

16 points per question

(1) A car traveled 70 kilometers in 2 hours. At what speed, in kilometers per hour, was the car traveling?

distance   time   speed

70 ÷ 2 = ☐

⟨Ans.⟩ _____ km/h

(2) A car traveled 90 km in 3 hours. At what speed, in kilometers per hour, was the car traveling?

⟨Ans.⟩ _____ km/h

© Kumon Publishing Co., Ltd.

2 Answer the following questions.

17 points per question

(1) Ritch rode his skateboard 1,800 meters in 10 minutes. At what speed, in meters per minute, was Ritch riding?

⟨Ans.⟩ _____ m/min

(2) Rachel ran 2,400 meters in 30 minutes. At what speed, in meters per minute, was she running?

⟨Ans.⟩ _____ m/min

3 Answer the following questions.

17 points per question

(1) A horse ran 120 meters in 8 seconds. What was the horse's speed in meters per second?

⟨Ans.⟩ _____ m/s

(2) Jacob ran 210 meters in 30 seconds. What was his speed in meters per second?

⟨Ans.⟩ _____ m/s

Unit Rates

Comparing Speeds

Review STEP 20

- A car traveled 120 kilometers in 3 hours. What was the car's speed in kilometers per hour?

⟨Ans.⟩ _____ km/h

1 **This morning, Ali, Ben, and Caitlyn ran across a field. The table on the right shows data about the distance and time each person ran.**

10 points per question

(1) Who was faster, Ali or Ben?

⟨Ans.⟩ _____

	This Morning's Run	
	Distance (meters)	Time (seconds)
Ali	100	20
Ben	80	20
Caitlyn	80	18

(2) Who was faster, Ben or Caitlyn?

⟨Ans.⟩ _____

(3) What was Ali's average speed? Answer in m/s.

$$\boxed{100} \div \boxed{20} = \boxed{}$$

⟨Ans.⟩ _____

(4) How many seconds did Caitlyn take to run 1 meter?

$$\boxed{18} \div \boxed{80} = \boxed{}$$

⟨Ans.⟩ _____

For these problems, assume each runner ran at a constant speed.

2 Car A travels 2,000 meters in 10 minutes. Car B travels 1,500 meters in 6 minutes. Which is faster? Compare how many meters they travel per minute.

20 points

distance   time   speed

Car A | 2,000 | ÷ | 10 | = | | m/min

Car B | | ÷ | | = | | m/min

⟨Ans.⟩ _____

3 Car A travels 150 kilometers in 2 hours. Car B travels 240 kilometers in 3 hours. Which is faster? Compare how many kilometers they travel per hour.

20 points

distance   time   speed

Car A | 150 | ÷ | 2 | = | | km/h

Car B | | ÷ | | = | | km/h

⟨Ans.⟩ _____

4 Rea can run 60 meters in 10 seconds. Felix can run 120 meters in 24 seconds. Who is faster? Compare how many meters they can run per second.

20 points

distance   time   speed

Rea | | ÷ | | = | | m/s

Felix | | ÷ | | = | | m/s

⟨Ans.⟩ _____

47

Converting Unit Rates

Review STEP 21

- Car A travels 3,000 meters in 15 minutes. Car B travels 2,000 meters in 8 minutes. Which is faster? Compare how many meters they travel per minute.

Car A

Car B

⟨Ans.⟩ _____

Don't Forget!

Some useful unit conversions for describing speed are
- 1 minute (min) = 60 seconds (s)
- 1 hour (h) = 60 minutes (min)
- 1 kilometer (km) = 1,000 meters (m)

1 Answer the following questions.

20 points per question

(1) Sound travels at a speed of 340 meters per second in air. What is its speed in meters per minute?

m/s		m/min

[   ] × 60 = [   ]   ⟨Ans.⟩ _____ m/min

(2) Jade rides at a speed of 6 meters per second. What is her speed in meters per minute?

⟨Ans.⟩ _____ m/min

(3) An airplane flies at a speed of 900 kilometers per hour. What is its speed in meters per minute?

m/h		m/min

[   ] ÷ 60 = [   ]   ⟨Ans.⟩ _____ m/min

2   A high-speed train travels 480 kilometers in 2 hours.

10 points

(1) What is the train's speed in kilometers per hour?

〈Ans.〉＿＿＿＿＿＿＿ km/h

(2) What is the train's speed in meters per minute?

15 points

240 km = ☐ m

1 hour = ☐ minutes

〈Ans.〉＿＿＿＿＿＿＿ m/min

(3) What is the train's speed in meters per second? Round the answer to the nearest whole number.

15 points

1 minute = ☐ seconds

4,000 ÷ ☐ = 66.6... ⟶ 67

〈Ans.〉＿＿＿＿＿＿＿ m/s

We converted km/h to m/min.
Then we converted m/min to m/s.

49

Calculating Distance

Review STEP 22

- A car travels 216 kilometers in 4 hours. What is its speed in meters per minute?

⟨Ans.⟩ _____ m/min

Don't Forget!

Recall the formula we used for finding speed. You can find distance by rearranging the formula.

$$\text{speed} \times \text{time} = \text{distance}$$

1 **A car travels at a speed of 40 kilometers per hour.**   15 points per question

(1) How far does the car travel in 2 hours?

speed		time		distance
	×		=	

⟨Ans.⟩ _____ km

(2) How far does the car travel in 3 hours?

⟨Ans.⟩ _____ km

(3) How far does the car travel in 4.5 hours?

⟨Ans.⟩ _____ km

2 **A train travels at a speed of 64 kilometers per hour.** 15 points per question

（1） How far does the train travel in 2 hours?

〈Ans.〉＿＿＿＿＿＿＿ km

（2） How far does the train travel in 2 hours and 30 minutes?

〈Ans.〉＿＿＿＿＿＿＿ km

3 **Sanjay went for a bike ride. He left at 7 a.m. and arrived at his destination at 10 a.m. He was riding at a speed of 12 kilometers per hour. How far away was his destination from his starting point?** 10 points

〈Ans.〉＿＿＿＿＿＿＿ km

4 **Alicia said "Yoo-hoo!" from an observation deck to the mountain across the valley. 6 seconds later, the echo came back to her. Sound travels through the air at a speed of 340 meters per second. What is the distance between the observation deck and the mountain?** 15 points

〈Ans.〉＿＿＿＿＿＿＿ m

mountain ← 3 seconds / 3 seconds → observation deck

51

Unit Rates
Calculating Time

Date / /

Score /100

Review STEP 23

- A train travels at a speed of 600 meters per minute. How far does the train travel in 5 minutes?

⟨Ans.⟩ _____ km

Don't Forget!

Recall the formula we used for finding speed. Time can be found by rearranging the formula.

$$\boxed{\text{distance} \div \text{speed} = \text{time}}$$

1 **Answer the following questions.**   15 points per question

(1) Kevin has 15 kilometers to hike today. If he hikes 3 kilometers per hour, how long will it take?

distance   speed   time
$\boxed{15} \div \boxed{3} = \boxed{}$

⟨Ans.⟩ _____ hours

(2) If he hikes 2 kilometers per hour, how long will it take?

⟨Ans.⟩ _____ hours

2 **Answer the following questions.**   15 points per question

（1） Maxine has 5.6 kilometers to drive. If she drives 700 meters per minute, how long will it take?

〈Ans.〉 _____ minutes

（2） Yuen has 5.6 kilometers to run. If he runs 500 meters per minute, how long will it take?

〈Ans.〉 _____ minutes

3 **Ann drove 24,000 meters at a speed of 15 kilometers per hour. How long did it take?**   10 points

〈Ans.〉 _____ hours

4 **A race car travels at a speed of 60 meters per second on a course of 5,820 meters per lap.**   15 points per question

（1） How many minutes and seconds does it take to complete one lap?

〈Ans.〉 _____ minute and _____ seconds

（2） What is the speed of the race car in kilometers per hour?

〈Ans.〉 _____ km/h

Review STEP 16 The table on the right shows data about two city parks, East Park and West Park. Which park is more crowded?
10 points

East Park

West Park

	City Parks	
	Area (m²)	Number of children
East Park	140	56
West Park	200	90

⟨Ans.⟩

Review STEP 17 Town A has an area of 38 square kilometers and a population of 7,824. Find the population density of this town. Round the answer to the nearest whole number.
10 points

⟨Ans.⟩ people/km²

Review STEP 18 Eva harvested 80 kilograms of potatoes from a field with an area of 25 square meters. Find the mass of potatoes per square meter.
10 points

⟨Ans.⟩ kg/m²

Review STEP 19 Frank is fertilizing his flower garden. He uses 0.4 kilograms of fertilizer for each 1 square meter of the garden.
10 points per question

(1) How many kilograms of fertilizer does he need for 7.2 square meters of the garden?

⟨Ans.⟩ kg

(2) If he has 1.2 kilograms of fertilizer, how many square meters of the garden can he fertilize?

⟨Ans.⟩ m²

Review **STEP 20** Mike drives 200 kilometers in 2.5 hours. What is his speed in kilometers per hour? 10 points

⟨Ans.⟩ _____ km/h

Review **STEP 21** **STEP 22** Sheila is riding her motorcycle at a speed of 30 kilometers per hour. What is her speed in meters per minute? 10 points

⟨Ans.⟩ _____ m/min

Review **STEP 23** A bus travels at a speed of 30 kilometers per hour. How far does the bus travel in 0.5 hours? 15 points

⟨Ans.⟩ _____ km

Review **STEP 24** Zoya drove 140 kilometers at a speed of 40 kilometers per hour. How long did it take? 15 points

⟨Ans.⟩ _____ hours

Review STEP 24

● Ann drove 21.6 kilometers at a speed of 12 meters per second. How many minutes did the drive take?

⟨Ans.⟩ _____ minutes

1 Answer the following questions. For each question, suppose we are creating our own unit of measurement. We'll call it the "base unit."

10 points per question

Example

A

Suppose we create our own unit of measurement. We'll call it the "base unit."
● If 1 base unit is equal to 1 centimeter (cm), what is the length of A in base units?
80 base units
● If 1 base unit is equal to 10 cm, what is the length of A in base units?
8 base units
● If 1 base unit is equal to 20 cm, what is the length of A in base units?
4 base units

(1) If 1 base unit is equal to 1 milliliter (mL), what is the volume of B in base units?

⟨Ans.⟩ _____ base units

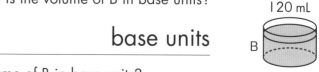

(2) If 1 base unit is equal to 2 mL, what is the volume of B in base units?

⟨Ans.⟩ _____ base units

(3) If 1 base unit is equal to 30 mL, what is the volume of B in base units?

⟨Ans.⟩ _____ base units

2 We will make a salad dressing by mixing 10 mL of vinegar and 15 mL of olive oil.

Vinegar   Olive oil

10 mL   15 mL

(1) If I base unit is equal to I mL, how many base units of vinegar will we need?　　　　　　　　　　　10 points

〈Ans.〉　　　　　　　base units

(2) If I base unit is equal to I mL, how many base units of olive oil will we need?　　　　　　　　　　　10 points

〈Ans.〉　　　　　　　base units

(3) If I base unit is equal to 5 mL, how many base units each of vinegar and olive oil will we need?

10 points for each blank

〈Ans.〉 vinegar:　　　　base units , olive oil:　　　　base units

(4) We want to make another batch of salad dressing with the same ratio of oil and vinegar as above. If we use 2 mL of vinegar, how many mL of olive oil would we use?　　　　　10 points

You can use question (3) to help you.

〈Ans.〉

(5) For another batch of salad dressing with the same ratio, if we use 30 mL of olive oil, how many mL of vinegar would we use?

10 points

〈Ans.〉

(6) What is the ratio of vinegar to olive oil in each batch of salad dressing we made? Write the ratio in the smallest whole numbers possible.

10 points

〈Ans.〉 The ratio is　　　　to　　　　.

STEP 26

Ratios and Proportions
Ratio Notation and Introducing
Common Denominators

Date / /

Score /100

Review STEP 25

● We made a salad dressing by mixing 30 mL of vinegar and 50 mL of olive oil. What is the ratio of vinegar to olive oil in this dressing? Write the smallest whole numbers possible.

⟨Ans.⟩ The ratio is _____ to _____ .

Don't Forget! Using the Colon

A ratio can be written using a colon—for example, 2 : 3.
We say this as "a ratio of two to three."

.2 cm.
3 cm

1 **Write the following ratios using a colon.**   10 points per question

(1) The ratio of volume A to volume B

A   B
5 mL   9 mL

⟨Ans.⟩ _____

(2) The ratio of boys to girls

5 boys   4 girls

⟨Ans.⟩ _____

(3) The ratio of length A to length B

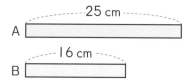

A ⟨----- 25 cm -----⟩

B ⟨-- 16 cm --⟩

⟨Ans.⟩ _____

2 Write the following ratios using a colon.

10 points per question

(1) String A is 8 centimeters long. String B is 17 centimeters long. What is the ratio of the length of A to the length of B?

⟨Ans.⟩ _____

(2) String A is 60 centimeters long. String B is 73 centimeters long. What is the ratio of the length of A to the length of B?

⟨Ans.⟩ _____

(3) String A is 4 meters long. String B is 15 meters long. What is the ratio of the length of A to the length of B?

⟨Ans.⟩ _____

3 For the questions below, suppose we are dividing strips A, B, C, and D into parts. Refer to the diagrams when answering the questions.

10 points per question

(1) Suppose that 1 part is 1 centimeter (cm).

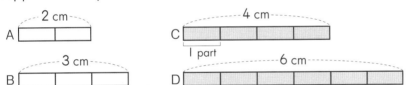

Write a ratio of A to B that indicates the number of parts.

⟨Ans.⟩ A : B = _____

Write a ratio of C to D that indicates the number of parts.

⟨Ans.⟩ C : D = _____

(2) Now suppose that 1 part is 2 centimeters.

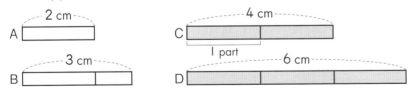

Write a ratio of C to D that indicates the number of parts.

⟨Ans.⟩ C : D = _____

(3) Using your answers to (1) and (2), are the ratios of A : B and C : D the same?

⟨Ans.⟩ _____

Review of Simplifying Fractions and Common Denominators

Don't Forget! Simplifying Fractions

- To **simplify** a fraction, divide the numerator (the top number) and the denominator (the bottom number) by the same number.

$$\div 2$$
$$\frac{2}{8} = \frac{1}{4}$$
$$\div 2$$

$\frac{2}{8}$ and $\frac{1}{4}$ have the same value.

(Divide top and bottom by 2)

$$\div 3$$
$$\frac{6}{9} = \frac{2}{3}$$
$$\div 3$$

$\frac{6}{9}$ and $\frac{2}{3}$ have the same value.

(Divide top and bottom by 3)

- When you simplify a fraction, you may be asked to simplify to **lowest terms**. That means to make sure the top and bottom numbers of the new fraction are the smallest whole numbers possible—they cannot be divided any further.

1 **Simplify by dividing the numerator and the denominator by 2.**

4 points per question

(1) $\frac{2}{6} = \frac{\boxed{1}}{3}$

(2) $\frac{6}{8} = \frac{\boxed{}}{4}$

(3) $\frac{2}{4} =$

(4) $\frac{4}{6} =$

(5) $\frac{8}{10} =$

2 **Simplify by dividing the numerator and the denominator by 3.**

4 points per question

(1) $\frac{3}{6} =$

(2) $\frac{3}{9} =$

(3) $\frac{9}{12} =$

(4) $\frac{6}{15} =$

(5) $\frac{15}{18} =$

3 **Simplify by dividing the numerator and the denominator by the same number. Simplify to lowest terms.**

4 points per question

(1) $\dfrac{5}{10} =$

(2) $\dfrac{7}{21} =$

(3) $\dfrac{4}{14} =$

(4) $\dfrac{4}{16} =$

(5) $\dfrac{8}{12} =$

(6) $\dfrac{6}{12} =$

(7) $\dfrac{10}{15} =$

(8) $\dfrac{12}{18} =$

(9) $\dfrac{16}{20} =$

Don't Forget!   Common Denominators

- When you find a **common denominator**, you change two fractions so they have the same denominator (bottom number) without changing the value of either fraction.
- The example shows two fractions modified to have the same common denominator. The lowest common denominator, 15, is used.

$\dfrac{2}{3}$ and $\dfrac{3}{5}$

$$\overset{\times 5}{\dfrac{2}{3} = \dfrac{10}{15}}\ \underset{\times 5}{}$$

$$\overset{\times 3}{\dfrac{3}{5} = \dfrac{9}{15}}\ \underset{\times 3}{}$$

4 **Find the lowest common denominator for each pair of fractions. Then write both fractions using that denominator.**

6 points per question

(1) $\left(\dfrac{1}{2},\ \dfrac{1}{4}\right) \longrightarrow \left(\dfrac{2}{4},\ \dfrac{1}{4}\right)$

(2) $\left(\dfrac{1}{6},\ \dfrac{1}{3}\right) \longrightarrow (\quad,\quad)$

(3) $\left(\dfrac{1}{3},\ \dfrac{1}{4}\right) \longrightarrow \left(\dfrac{4}{12},\ \dfrac{3}{12}\right)$

(4) $\left(\dfrac{2}{5},\ \dfrac{3}{4}\right) \longrightarrow (\quad,\quad)$

STEP **27**

Ratios and Proportions

Introducing Proportionality

Date / /

Score

/100

Review STEP 26

- String A is 27 centimeters long. String B is 16 centimeters long. What is the ratio of the length of A to the length of B?

〈Ans.〉 A : B = _____

Don't Forget!

- Recall that a **ratio** shows how large or small one value is in comparison to another.
- A ratio can be expressed as a comparison of two values using division. In the diagram, the ratio of the length of A to the length of B can be written in various ways, such as $2 : 3$, $2 \div 3$, or $\frac{2}{3}$.

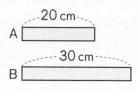

1 **Write each ratio as a fraction. Simplify to lowest terms.**

12 points per question

(1) $1 : 3 \left(\frac{1}{3} \right)$ (2) $4 : 6 \left(\frac{2}{3} \right)$ (3) $9 : 12 \left(\right)$

(4) $24 : 26 \left(\right)$ (5) $28 : 35 \left(\right)$

Don't Forget!   Proportional Ratios

- If two ratios have the same value, the ratios are **proportional**.

$$2 : 3 \rightarrow \frac{2}{3}$$

$$4 : 6 \rightarrow \frac{2}{3}$$

$$2 : 3 = 4 : 6$$

> 2 : 3 and 4 : 6 are proportional.

- The retangles shown to the right are a visual example of proportional ratios. The heights and widths of the rectangles are different.
But the ratio of height to width for each rectangle has the same value.

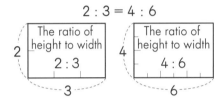

2 : 3 = 4 : 6

---

2 **For each question, choose the correct answer from the box.**

10 points per question

(1) Which ratio is proportional to 1 : 3?

⟨Ans.⟩ _____

2 : 4	2 : 5
2 : 6	2 : 7

(2) Which ratio is proportional to 3 : 5?

⟨Ans.⟩ _____

4 : 6	6 : 8
8 : 10	9 : 15

(3) Which ratio is proportional to 5 : 2?

⟨Ans.⟩ _____

12 : 4	20 : 12
10 : 6	15 : 6

(4) Which ratio is proportional to 3 : 4?

⟨Ans.⟩ _____

15 : 24	12 : 20
21 : 28	25 : 50

Review STEP 27

● Write the following ratios as fractions. Simplify to the lowest terms.

$4:6$ ( ) $6:9$ ( )

Don't Forget!

● For a ratio $\triangle : \bigcirc$, if you multiply or divide $\triangle$ and $\bigcirc$ by the same number, the new ratio is **proportional** to the original. This can be shown by using an equal sign, as below.

$$2:3=4:6$$

$$\overset{\times 2}{2:3}=4:6 \qquad \overset{\div 2}{4:6}=2:3$$

$$\underset{\times 2}{2:3}=4:6 \qquad \underset{\div 2}{4:6}=2:3$$

● A pair of equal ratios connected by an equal sign is called a **proportion**.

1 **Fill in the boxes.**

10 points per question

(1)
$$1:2=2:4$$
$\times \square$ (top), $\times \square$ (bottom)

(2)
$$4:3=8:6$$
$\times \square$ (top), $\times \square$ (bottom)

(3)
$$5:2=15:6$$
$\times \square$ (top), $\times \square$ (bottom)

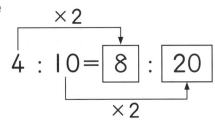

STEP 1-2
Rounding

STEP 3-6
Introduction to Ratios

STEP 7-15
Percentages

STEP 16-24
Unit Rates

STEP 25-40
Ratios and Proportions

STEP 41-47
Analyzing Data

STEP 48-53
Number of Possible Outcomes

Example

×2

$4 : 10 = \boxed{8} : \boxed{20}$

×2

÷2

$4 : 10 = \boxed{2} : \boxed{5}$

÷2

2 **Multiply or divide both parts of the ratio by the same number to complete the proportion.**

7 points per question

(1)

×2

$2 : 6 = \boxed{4} : \boxed{}$

×2

(2)

÷2

$2 : 6 = \boxed{} : \boxed{3}$

÷2

(3)

×3

$2 : 4 = \boxed{} : \boxed{}$

(4)

÷2

$2 : 4 = \boxed{} : \boxed{}$

(5)

÷6

$12 : 24 = \boxed{} : \boxed{}$

(6)

$12 : 24 = \boxed{} : \boxed{}$

×3

(7)

÷10

$40 : 30 = \boxed{} : \boxed{}$

(8)

$40 : 30 = \boxed{} : \boxed{}$

×2

(9)

÷5

$5 : 25 = \boxed{} : \boxed{}$

(10)

$5 : 25 = \boxed{} : \boxed{}$

×4

Make sure you multiply or divide both parts of the ratio by the same number.

Writing Proportions

Review STEP 28

● Fill in the boxes to complete the proportion.

$$\overset{\div 3}{\overbrace{}}$$

$15 : 6 = \boxed{} : \boxed{}$

$$\overset{\times 8}{\overbrace{}}$$

$5 : 4 = \boxed{} : \boxed{}$

1 **Fill in the box to complete the proportion.**

8 points per question

Example

$2 : 5 = 4 : \boxed{}$ ➡ $2 : 5 = 4 : \boxed{10}$ $\overset{\times 2}{\overbrace{}}$ $\underset{\times 2}{\underbrace{}}$

(1)

$1 : 3 = 4 : \boxed{}$

(2)

$3 : 4 = 9 : \boxed{}$

(3)

$4 : 3 = \boxed{} : 12$

(4)

$3 : 7 = \boxed{} : 21$

(5)

$6 : 5 = \boxed{} : 30$

2 Fill in the box to complete the proportion.

6 points per question

(1)

$$9 : 12 = 3 : \boxed{}$$

(2)

$$8 : 12 = 2 : \boxed{}$$

(3)

$$16 : 12 = 4 : \boxed{}$$

(4)

$$6 : 8 = \boxed{} : 4$$

(5)

$$18 : 12 = \boxed{} : 2$$

(6)

$$27 : 18 = \boxed{} : 2$$

Don't Forget!

To simplify a ratio of whole numbers, you divide both numbers of the ratio by the same whole number so that both numbers are the lowest whole numbers possible.

3 Simplify each ratio to lowest terms.

8 points per question

(1) $8 : 6$

⟨Ans.⟩ _____

(2) $18 : 42$

⟨Ans.⟩ _____

(3) $14 : 49$

⟨Ans.⟩ _____

Ratios and Proportions
Simplifying Ratios Involving Decimals and Fractions

Date   /   /

Score

/100

Review STEP 29

● Fill in the empty box to complete the proportion.

$$20 : 15 = \boxed{} : 3 \qquad 12 : 21 = 4 : \boxed{}$$

1 Simplify each ratio to lowest terms.

10 points per question

Example

Simplify the ratio to lowest terms.   0.9 : 1.5

Multiply both sides by 10 to change decimals to whole numbers.

$$0.9 : 1.5 = 9 : 15$$

Then simplify.

$$9 : 15 = 3 : 5$$

(1) $0.5 : 0.6 = \boxed{5} : \boxed{}$

(2) $0.8 : 2.4 = \boxed{8} : \boxed{} = \boxed{} : \boxed{}$

(3) $0.9 : 1.2 = \boxed{} : \boxed{} = \boxed{} : \boxed{}$

2 Simplify each ratio to lowest terms.

10 points per question

Example

Simplify the ratio to lowest terms. $\frac{2}{3} : \frac{4}{5}$

Convert fractions to have a common denominator.

$$\frac{2}{3} : \frac{4}{5} = \frac{10}{15} : \frac{12}{15}$$

Convert fractions to whole numbers.

$$\frac{10}{15} : \frac{12}{15} = 10 : 12$$

Then simplify to lowest terms.

$$10 : 12 = 5 : 6$$

(1) $\dfrac{1}{2} : \dfrac{3}{5} = \dfrac{5}{10} : \dfrac{6}{10} = 5 : 6$

(2) $\dfrac{2}{3} : \dfrac{3}{4} = \dfrac{8}{12} : \boxed{} = \boxed{} : \boxed{}$

(3) $\dfrac{5}{6} : \dfrac{2}{9} = \dfrac{15}{18} : \boxed{} = 15 : \boxed{}$

(4) $\dfrac{3}{8} : \dfrac{3}{5} = \dfrac{15}{40} : \boxed{} = 15 : \boxed{} = \boxed{} : \boxed{}$

(5) $\dfrac{12}{5} : 6 = \boxed{} : \dfrac{30}{5} = \boxed{} : \boxed{} = \boxed{} : \boxed{}$

(6) $\dfrac{4}{9} : \dfrac{5}{12} =$

(7) $\dfrac{3}{8} : \dfrac{5}{14} =$

Problem Solving with Proportions

Review STEP 30

- Simplify each ratio to lowest terms.

(1) $0.9 : 1.5 =$

(2) $\dfrac{2}{3} : \dfrac{4}{5} =$

---

1 **Answer the following questions.**

10 points each for A and B

Example

You're making a cake, and the ratio of flour to sugar is 5 : 2.
If you use 150 grams of flour, how much sugar do you need?

(*Method A*) Let the amount of sugar be x grams.

$$\overset{\times 30}{5 : 2 = 150 : x} \longrightarrow x = 2 \times 30 = 60$$
$$\underset{\times 30}{}$$

⟨Ans.⟩ _____ 60 g

(*Method B*) The amount of sugar equals $\dfrac{2}{5}$ of the amount of flour.

$$150 \times \dfrac{2}{5} = 60$$

⟨Ans.⟩ _____ 60 g

You're making a cake, and the ratio of flour to sugar is 5 : 3.
If you use 150 grams of flour, how much sugar do you need?

(Method A)
Let the amount of sugar be x grams.

$$5 : 3 = \boxed{} : x$$

$$x = \boxed{} \times \boxed{} = \boxed{}$$

⟨Ans.⟩ _____

(Method B)
The amount of sugar equals $\dfrac{3}{5}$ of the amount of flour.

$$150 \times \boxed{\dfrac{3}{5}} =$$

⟨Ans.⟩ _____

2 **You are drawing a rectangle, and you want the ratio of width to length to be 5 : 8. If the width is 45 centimeters, what is the length?**

10 points each for A and B

(Method A)
Let the length be x cm.

$$5 : 8 = \boxed{} : x$$

$$x = \boxed{} \times \boxed{9} = \boxed{}$$

⟨Ans.⟩ _____

(Method B)
The length equals 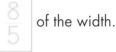 of the width.

$$45 \times \boxed{} =$$

⟨Ans.⟩ _____

3 **Find the value of x.**

20 points per question

(1) $5 : 2 = x : 10$

⟨Ans.⟩ _____

(2) $16 : 12 = 4 : x$

⟨Ans.⟩ _____

(3) $7.5 : 5 = 3 : x$

⟨Ans.⟩ _____

Ratios and Proportions

Date / /

Score

/100

Review STEP 25

Answer the questions about the following scenario: A recipe for salad dressing calls for 5 milliliters of vinegar and 15 milliliters of olive oil. 7 points per question

(1) Suppose we create our own unit of measurement called a "base unit." If 1 base unit is equal to 1 milliliter, how many base units of vinegar would we need to make the dressing?

⟨Ans.⟩ _____ base unit(s)

(2) If 1 base unit is equal to 5 milliliters, how many base units each of vinegar and olive oil would we need to make the dressing?

⟨Ans.⟩ vinegar : _____ base unit(s), olive oil : _____ base unit(s)

Review STEP 26

Write the following ratios using a colon. 7 points per question

(1) String A is 7 centimeters long. String B is 16 centimeters long. What is the ratio of the length of A to the length of B?

⟨Ans.⟩ _____

(2) String A is 5 centimeters long. String B is 17 centimeters long. What is the ratio of the length of A to the length of B?

⟨Ans.⟩ _____

Review STEP 27

Choose the correct answer from the box. 8 points

Which ratio is proportional to 2 : 3?

⟨Ans.⟩ _____

| 4 : 5 | 6 : 8 |
| 4 : 6 | 8 : 15 |

Review **STEP 28** Fill in the boxes to complete the proportion.

8 points per question

(1) $2 : 5 = \boxed{} : \boxed{}$

$\underset{\times 2}{\underline{}}$

(2) $4 : 10 = \boxed{} : \boxed{}$

$\underset{\div 2}{\underline{}}$

Review **STEP 29** Fill in the box to complete the proportion.

8 points per question

(1) $1 : 5 = 5 : \boxed{}$

(2) $20 : 16 = \boxed{} : 4$

Review **STEP 30** Simplify each ratio to lowest common terms.

8 points per question

(1) $0.5 : 0.8 =$

(2) $\dfrac{2}{3} : \dfrac{4}{5} =$

Review **STEP 31** Find the value of x.

8 points per question

(1) $5 : 3 = x : 6$

⟨Ans.⟩ _____

(2) $18 : 12 = 3 : x$

⟨Ans.⟩ _____

Review STEP 31

- Find the value of x.

(1) $15 : 6 = x : 2$ ⟨Ans.⟩ _____

(2) $6 : 24 = 3 : x$ ⟨Ans.⟩ _____

Don't Forget!   Directly Proportional Relationships

- Suppose a sink is filling up with water at a rate of 2 liters per minute. The table shows the relationship between time and volume of water in the sink.

Time (min) x	1	2	3	4	5	6	...
Volume of water (L) y	2	4	6	8	10	12	...

×3
×2

×2
×3

- As time (x) doubles or triples, the volume of water in the sink (y) doubles or triples. This is because the volume of water is increasing in **direct proportion** to time.

1 **Answer the questions involving the table below. The table shows the perimeter (the total distance around the outside) of a square in relation to the length of one side of the square.** 10 points per question

(1) Complete the table by filling in the missing information.

Side Length and Perimeter of a Square

Side length (cm) x	1	2	3	...
Perimeter (cm) y	4	8		...

(2) When side length (x) is doubled from 1 to 2, how does perimeter (y) change?

⟨Ans.⟩ _____

(3) When x is tripled, how does y change?

⟨Ans.⟩ _____

(4) For squares, is perimeter directly proportional to side length?

⟨Ans.⟩ _____

2 For each question, read the description and complete the table. Then determine whether the relationship indicated is directly proportional.

8 points per table, 4 points per ⟨Ans.⟩

(1) A sink fills with water at a rate of 3 liters per minute.

Time (min)	x	1	2	3	4	5	6	7	···
Volume of water (L)	y	3	6	9					···

Is the relationship between time and volume directly proportional? ⟨Ans.⟩

(2) A parent is 24 years old when their child is born.

Parent's age	x	24	25	26					···
Child's age	y	0	1	2					···

Is the relationship between the parent's age and the child's age directly proportional? ⟨Ans.⟩

(3) A 24-centimeter string will be cut into pieces of equal length.

Number of pieces	x	1	2	3	4	5	6	···
Length of each piece (cm)	y	24	12	8				···

Is the relationship between number of pieces and length directly proportional? ⟨Ans.⟩

(4) A train is traveling at 80 kilometers per hour.

Time traveled (h)	x	1	2	3	4				···
Distance traveled (km)	y	80							···

Is the relationship between time and distance directly proportional? ⟨Ans.⟩

(5) A piece of rope has a mass of 40 grams for every 10 centimeters in length.

Length of piece of rope (cm)	x	10	20	30				···
Mass of piece of rope (g)	y	40						···

Is the relationship between length and mass directly proportional? ⟨Ans.⟩

75

STEP **33**

Ratios and Proportions

Directly Proportional Relationships

Date / /

Score

/100

Review STEP 32

- Each table shows data about a tub filling with water. Study each table and answer the question below it.

(1)

Time (min) x	2	4	6	8	⋯
Depth of water (cm) y	10	20	30	40	⋯

Is the relationship between time and depth directly proportional? 〈Ans.〉 _____

(2)

Time (min) x	2	4	6	8	⋯
Depth of water (cm) y	10	15	20	30	⋯

Is the relationship between time and depth directly proportional? 〈Ans.〉 _____

Don't Forget!

- If the relationship between x and y is directly proportional, you will always get a fixed value (the same value) when you divide any value of y by the corresponding value of x.

$$y \div x = \text{fixed value}$$

(The same is true if you divide any value of x by the corresponding value of y.)
- The following equation, based on the relationship above, is also true.

$$y = \text{fixed value} \times x$$

1 **The table shows the relationship between time and volume for a rectangular sink that is filling up with water. Study the table and answer the questions below.**

10 points per question

Time (min) x	1	2	3	4	5	6	⋯
Volume of water (L) y	4	8	12	16	20	24	⋯
$y \div x$	4						⋯

(1) Fill in the missing information in the bottom row of the table.

(2) Complete the number sentence to show a relationship between x and y. $y \div x = \boxed{}$

(3) Write the appropriate number in the number sentence. $y = \boxed{} \times x$

2 In each table, the relationship between x and y is directly proportional. Complete the number sentences below.

15 points per question

(1)

x	1	2	3	4	5	6	7	$\cdots$
y	2	4	6	8	10	12	14	$\cdots$
$y \div x$	2	2	2	2				

⟨Ans.⟩ $y = \boxed{} \times x$

(2)

x	1	2	3	4	5	$\cdots$
y	30	60	90	120	150	$\cdots$
$y \div x$	30					

⟨Ans.⟩ $y = \boxed{} \times x$

3 The table shows the relationship between the length of a piece of steel wire and its mass. Study the table and answer the questions.

10 points per question

Length of piece of wire (m) x	1	2	3	4	5	6	$\cdots$
Mass of piece of wire (g) y	7	14	21	28	35	42	$\cdots$

(1) When you divide mass (y) by length (x), what is the resulting value?

⟨Ans.⟩ The mass per $\boxed{}$ meter of wire

(2) Does the mass of a piece of wire change in direct proportion to its length?

⟨Ans.⟩ _____

(3) Complete the number sentence to show a relationship between x and y.

⟨Ans.⟩ $y = $ _____

(4) When x is 12 m, how much is y?

⟨Ans.⟩ _____

© Kumon Publishing Co., Ltd.

Ratios and Proportions
Directionality in Directly Proportional Relationships

Date / /

Score /100

Review STEP **33**

● Emma buys wire at a rate of 5 dollars per meter. Write a number sentence that shows the relationship between length (x) and cost (y) in this situation.

⟨Ans.⟩ $y =$ _____

Don't Forget!

In a table showing a directly proportional relationship, the values are related in either direction—not just from left to right, but also from right to left. In the example below, going from right to left, if x is multiplied by $\frac{1}{2}$, y is multiplied by $\frac{1}{2}$ too.

x	1	2	3	4	5	···
y	4	8	12	16	20	···

1 The table below shows data about time and depth of water in a sink. The relationship is directly proportional.

10 points per ☐

Time (min) x	1	2	3	4	5	6	7	8	9	···
Depth (cm) y	4	8	12	16	20	24	28	32	36	···

How do x and y change from the start of arrow A to the end? (Note the direction of the arrow.) How about for arrow B?

(A) x (multiplied by ☐) y (multiplied by ☐)

(B) x (multiplied by ☐) y (multiplied by ☐)

2 **The table below shows the relationship between the number of paper bills in a stack and their total mass.**

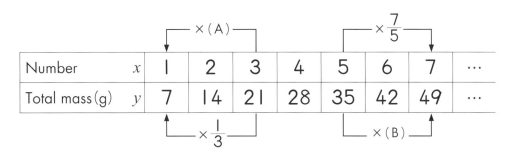

(1) Is the mass proportional to the number of bills?   10 points

⟨Ans.⟩ _____

(2) Find the value of A and B.   5 points per ☐

(A) [ ]   (B) [ ]
⟨Ans.⟩ _____

(3) Write a number sentence that shows the relationship between x and y.   10 points

⟨Ans.⟩ $y =$ _____

(4) Find the value of y given these values of x.   10 points per question

$x = 0$ $y = 7 \times 0 =$

⟨Ans.⟩ _____

$x = 15$

⟨Ans.⟩ _____

(5) When y is 364, what is the value of x?   10 points

⟨Ans.⟩ _____

Graphing Directly Proportional Relationships

Review STEP **34**

● Answer the following questions, where x is time and y is the distance traveled by a ship moving at 9 meters per second.

(1) Write a number sentence that shows the relationship between x and y.

⟨Ans.⟩ $y =$ _____

(2) If x is 150, what is the value of y?

⟨Ans.⟩ _____

Don't Forget! Graph of a Directly Proportional Relationship

The graph of a directly proportional relationship is a diagonal line that passes through the point (0, 0).

1 **The table on the left shows the relationship between time (x) and the depth of water (y) as Jarrett fills a sink. The relationship is directly proportional. Use the table to complete the graph on the right.**

30 points

Time and Depth of Water

Time (min) x	1	2	3	4	5	6	...
Depth (cm) y	5	10	15	20	25	30	...

Draw dots on the grid to represent each x and y pair. Then connect the dots with a line passing through the point (0, 0).

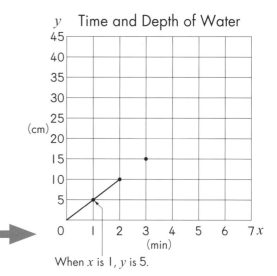

y Time and Depth of Water

When x is 1, y is 5.

2 Alan is riding his bicycle at a constant speed of 0.2 kilometers per minute. The distance (y) and the time (x) are directly proportional. Use the table to draw the graph below.

30 points

Time and Distance Alan Traveled

Time (min)	x	0	1	2	3	4	5	6	7	···
Distance (km)	y	0	0.2	0.4	0.6	0.8	1	1.2	1.4	···

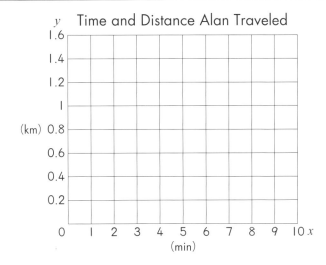

3 A certain kind of metal wire costs 150 dollars per meter. The total cost (y) and the total length (x) are directly proportional.

20 points per question

(1) Write a number sentence that shows the relationship between x and y.

⟨Ans.⟩ $y = $ _____

(2) Draw a graph of the relationship between x and y.

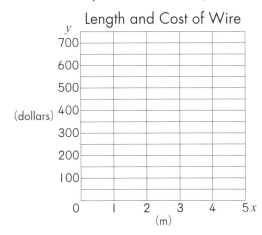

STEP **36**

Ratios and Proportions
· ·
**Comparing Graphs of Directly
Proportional Relationships**

Date / /

Score

/100

Review STEP **35**

● In an equilateral triangle, the length of one side (x) is directly proportional to the triangle's perimeter (y). Draw a graph of the relationship between side length and perimeter.

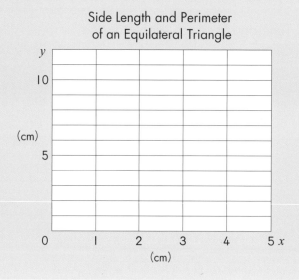

Side Length and Perimeter
of an Equilateral Triangle

1 **Answer the following questions based on the graph below.**

10 points per question

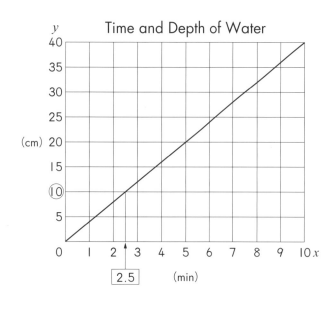

Time and Depth of Water

Example

When x is 2.5, y is 10.

(1) When x is 7.5, what is the value of y?

⟨**Ans.**⟩ _____

(2) When y is 40, what is the value of x?

⟨**Ans.**⟩ _____

STEP 1-2
Rounding

STEP 3-6
Introduction to
Ratios

STEP 7-15
Percentages

STEP 16-24
Unit Rates

STEP 25-40
Ratios and
Proportions

STEP 41-47
Analyzing Data

STEP 48-53
Number of
Possible
Outcomes

2 **The graph below shows the time and distance run by Anita and Ben in the first 10 minutes of a race.**

20 points per question

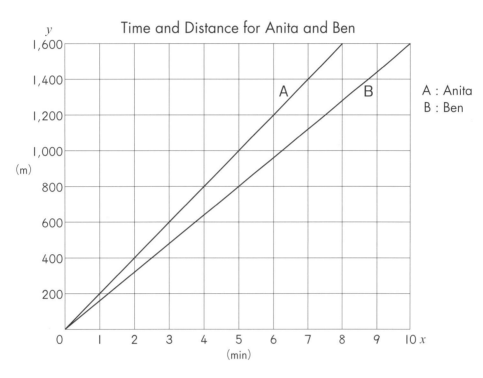

(1) How far did Anita run in 5 minutes?

⟨Ans.⟩ _____

(2) How far did Ben run in 5 minutes?

⟨Ans.⟩ _____

(3) Who is faster, Anita or Ben?

⟨Ans.⟩ _____

(4) Five minutes after the start, how far is Anita from Ben?

⟨Ans.⟩ _____

STEP **37**

Ratios and Proportions
···
Introduction to Inversely Proportional Relationships

Date   /   /

Score   /100

Review STEP 36

- The graph on the right shows the relationship between time (x, in minutes) and the depth (y, in centimeters) when Steve is filling a sink with water.

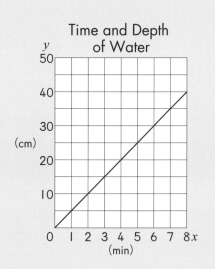

Time and Depth of Water

(1) By how much does the depth of the water increase each minute?

〈Ans.〉 _____

(2) How long does it take Steve to fill the sink to a depth of 20 centimeters?

〈Ans.〉 _____

Don't Forget!   Inverse Proportions

- The table below shows the relationship between the possible length (x) and possible width (y) of a rectangle with an area of 18 square centimeters (cm^2).

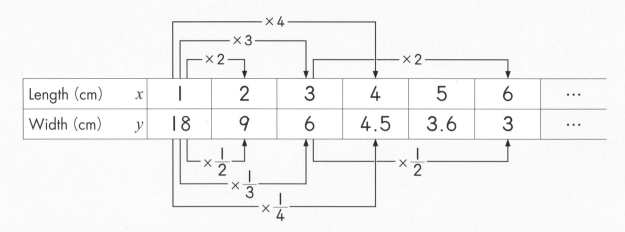

Length (cm)	x	1	2	3	4	5	6	⋯
Width (cm)	y	18	9	6	4.5	3.6	3	⋯

- When length (x) is multiplied by 2 or 3, width (y) is multiplied by $\frac{1}{2}$ or $\frac{1}{3}$. This is because the relationship between the values is **inversely proportional**.

1 **For each question, read the description and complete the table. Then determine whether the relationship indicated is directly proportional, inversely proportional, or neither.**

10 points per table, 15 points for ⟨Ans.⟩

(1) A container is being filled with water at a rate of 2 liters per minute.

×3

Time (min)	x	1	2	3	4	5	6	⋯
Volume (L)	y	2	4					⋯

× ☐

Is the relationship between time and volume directly proportional, inversely proportional, or neither?　　⟨Ans.⟩ _____

(2) You want to draw a rectangle that has an area of 24 square centimeters.

×3

Length of rectangle (cm)	x	1	2	3	4	5	6	⋯
Width of rectangle (cm)	y	24	12			4.8		⋯

× ☐

Is the relationship between length and width directly proportional, inversely proportional, or neither?　　⟨Ans.⟩ _____

(3) You want to draw a rectangle with a perimeter of 18 centimeters.

×3

Length of rectangle (cm)	x	1	2	3	4	5	6	⋯
Width of rectangle (cm)	y	8	7					⋯

× ☐

Is the relationship between length and width directly proportional, inversely proportional, or neither?　　⟨Ans.⟩ _____

(4) You want to draw a parallelogram with an area of 36 square centimeters.

×3

Height of parallelogram (cm)	x	1	2	3	4	5	6	⋯
Base of parallelogram (cm)	y	36				7.2		⋯

× ☐

Is the relationship between height and base directly proportional, inversely proportional, or neither?　　⟨Ans.⟩ _____

STEP **38**

Ratios and Proportions
Inversely Proportional Relationships

Date / /

Score

/100

Review STEP 37

● Indicate whether each relationship is directly proportional or inversely proportional.

(1) The height and base of a parallelogram with an area of 36 cm²

Height (cm) x	1	2	3	...
Base (cm) y	36	18	12	...

⟨Ans.⟩ _____

(2) Time and volume when filling a large container with water

Time (min) x	1	2	3	...
Volume (L) y	5	10	15	...

⟨Ans.⟩ _____

Don't Forget!

When y is inversely proportional to x, the product of x and y is always the same.

$$x \times y = \text{fixed number}$$ $$y = \text{fixed number} \div x$$

1 You want to draw a rectangle with an area of 24 square centimeters. The table below shows the relationship between length (x) and width (y) for the rectangle.

(1)10 points, (2)10 points per ☐

(1) Fill in the missing information in the table.

Length (cm) x	1	2	3	4	5	6	...
Width (cm) y	24	12	8	6	4.8	4	...
$x \times y$							

(2) Complete the number sentences below.

$$x \times y = \boxed{} \qquad y = \boxed{} \div x$$

2 **In the questions below, y is inversely proportional to x. Complete the number sentences.**

<u>15 points per question</u>

(1)

x	1	2	3	4	5	...
y	12	6	4	3	2.4	...
$x \times y$	12	12				

⟨Ans.⟩ $y = \boxed{} \div x$

(2)

x	1	2	3	4	5	...
y	18	9	6	4.5	3.6	...
$x \times y$	18					

⟨Ans.⟩ $y = \boxed{} \div x$

3 **The table below shows the relationship between average speed in kilometers per hour (km/h) and total time in hours (h) for a 120-kilometer trip.**

<u>10 points per question</u>

Average speed (km/h) x	20	30	40	50	60	...
Total time (h) y	6	4	3	2.4	2	...

(1) What does the product of x and y represent?

⟨Ans.⟩ _____

(2) Is the total time inversely proportional to the speed?

⟨Ans.⟩ _____

(3) Write a number sentence that shows the relationship between x and y.

⟨Ans.⟩ $y = $ _____

(4) If x is 48, what is the value of y?

⟨Ans.⟩ _____

Review STEP 38

- Suppose that y is inversely proportional to x. When x is 1, y is 24. When x is 12, what is the value of y?

⟨Ans.⟩ _____

Don't Forget!

When y is inversely proportional to x, if x is halved or divided by three, y is doubled or tripled.

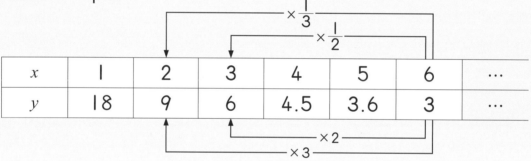

1 How do x and y change from the start of arrow **A** to the end? (Note the direction of the arrow.) How about for arrow **B**?

10 points per ☐

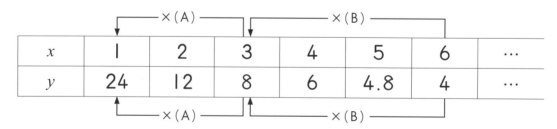

(A) x (multiplied by ☐) y (multiplied by ☐)

(B) x (multiplied by ☐) y (multiplied by ☐)

2 The table below shows the relationship between average speed in kilometers per hour (km/h) and total time in hours (h) for a 180-kilometer trip.

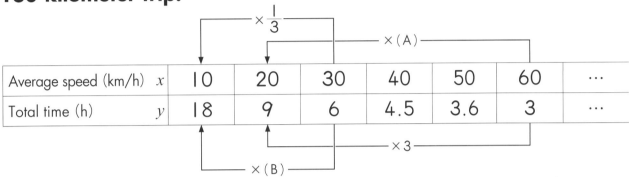

Average speed (km/h) x	10	20	30	40	50	60	...
Total time (h) y	18	9	6	4.5	3.6	3	...

(1) Find the values of A and B.

10 points per ☐

⟨Ans.⟩ (A) ☐   (B) ☐

(2) Write a number sentence that shows the relationship between x and y.

10 points

⟨Ans.⟩ $y =$ _____

(3) Find the value of y given these values of x.

10 points per question

$x = 5$ $y = \boxed{} \div 5 =$

⟨Ans.⟩ _____

$x = 15$

⟨Ans.⟩ _____

(4) When y is 1.8, what is the value of x?

10 points

⟨Ans.⟩ _____

STEP **40**

Ratios and Proportions
Graphing Inversely
Proportional Relationships

Date / /

Score

/100

Review STEP 39

● y is inversely proportional to x. When x is 2, y is 5.

(1) Write a number sentence that shows the relationship between x and y.

⟨Ans.⟩ $y =$ _____

(2) When x is 4, what is the value of y?

⟨Ans.⟩ _____

Don't Forget! Graph of an Inversely Proportional Relationship

Graphs that show the relationship between inversely proportional values have a smooth curve.

1 **Complete the graph on the right using the table on the left.** 50 points

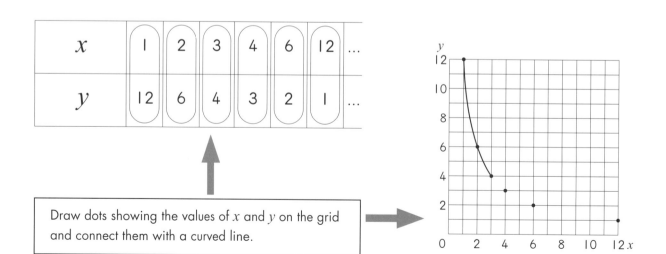

x	1	2	3	4	6	12	...
y	12	6	4	3	2	1	...

Draw dots showing the values of x and y on the grid and connect them with a curved line.

2 **The table shows the relationship between length and width for a rectangle with an area of 24 square centimeters. Use the table to draw the graph.**

50 points

Length and Width for a Rectangle with an Area of 24 Square Centimeters

| Length (cm) x | 1 | 2 | 3 | 4 | 5 | 6 | 8 | 12 | 24 | ⋯ |
| Width (cm) y | 24 | 12 | 8 | 6 | 4.8 | 4 | 3 | 2 | 1 | ⋯ |

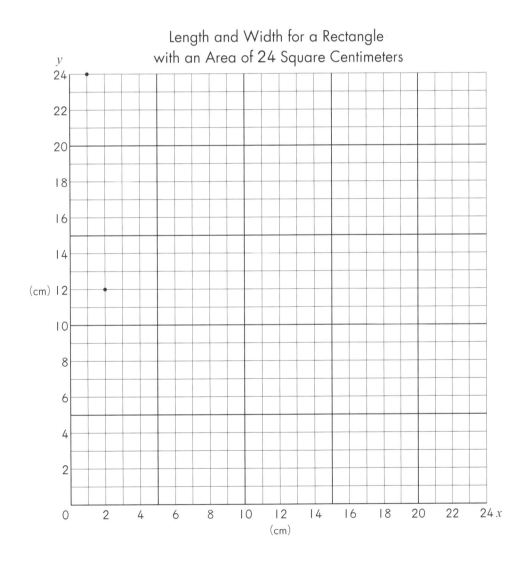

Length and Width for a Rectangle with an Area of 24 Square Centimeters

Ratios and Proportions

Date	/	/
Score		/100

Review STEP 32 · **Answer the questions using the information below.**

7 points per question

A sink fills with water at a rate of 2 liters per minute.

Time (min)	x	1	2	3	4	5	6	7	...
Volume of water (L)	y	2	4						...

(1) Fill in the missing information in the table.

(2) When x is doubled, how does y change?

⟨Ans.⟩ _____

(3) When x is multiplied by 4, what happens to y?

⟨Ans.⟩ _____

(4) Is the relationship between time and volume directly proportional?

⟨Ans.⟩ _____

Review STEP 33 STEP 34 · **The table shows the relationship between time and volume for a sink that is filling up with water. Write a number sentence to show the relationship between x and y.**

7 points

Time (min)	x	1	2	3	4	5	6	...
Volume (L)	y	4	8	12	16	20	24	...

⟨Ans.⟩ $y =$ _____

Review STEP 35 STEP 36 · **Use the graph to answer the questions.**

8 points per question

(1) When x is 3, what is the value of y?

⟨Ans.⟩ _____

(2) When y is 600, what is the value of x?

⟨Ans.⟩ _____

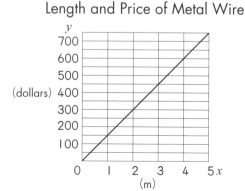

Length and Price of Metal Wire

Review STEP 37 Answer the questions involving the table below.

7 points per question

The table shows the relationship between length and width for rectangles with an area of 18 square centimeters.

Length (cm)	x	1	2	3	4	5	...
Width (cm)	y	18					...

(1) Fill in the missing information.

(2) When x is doubled, how does the value of y change?

⟨Ans.⟩ _____

(3) When y is divided by 4, how does the value of x change?

⟨Ans.⟩ _____

(4) Is the relationship between length and width inversely proportional?

⟨Ans.⟩ _____

Review STEP 38 – STEP 40 The table below shows the relationship between average speed and total time for an 840-meter trip.

7 points per question

Average speed (m/min)	x	40	50	60	70	80	...
Total time of trip (min)	y	21	16.8	14	12	10.5	...

(1) What does the product of x and y represent?

⟨Ans.⟩ _____

(2) Write a number sentence that shows the relationship between x and y.

⟨Ans.⟩ $y =$ _____

(3) If x is 30, what is the value of y?

⟨Ans.⟩ _____

STEP **41**

Analyzing Data
....

Introduction to the Mean

Date / /

Score /100

Review STEP **40**

- Use the graph to answer the questions below.

When x is 2, what is y? ☐

When y is 1, what is x? ☐

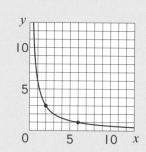

Don't Forget!   Finding the Mean

The **mean** is an average of a set of values.

> mean = the sum of the values ÷ the number of values

1   **There are 4 containers of liquid, as shown below. Answer the following questions.**

15 points total for (1) and (2)

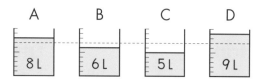

A   B   C   D
8 L   6 L   5 L   9 L

(1)   How could you adjust the volume of liquid in each container so that the volume in each container will be the same? Fill in the blanks below.

• Move ☐ 1 ☐ liter from A to B so both containers have ☐ 7 ☐ liters.

• Move ☐ liters from D to C so both containers have ☐ liters.

(2)   Use the formula above to calculate the mean volume of the liquid in the containers. Compare your answer to your responses in the previous question.

$$\left(\boxed{8} + \boxed{6} + \boxed{} + \boxed{} \right) \div \boxed{} = \boxed{} \ \text{L}$$

2 You have 4 apples. The mass of each apple is given below, in grams (g). Answer the following questions. 15 points per question

241 g   244 g   246 g   249 g

(1) Find the total mass of the 4 apples.

⟨Ans.⟩ _____

(2) What is the mean mass of the apples?

sum ÷ number of apples = mean

⟨Ans.⟩ _____

3 A hen laid 7 eggs. The mass of each egg is given below. 20 points

55 g, 56 g, 54 g, 55 g, 58 g, 53 g, 54 g
What is the mean mass of the eggs?

⟨Ans.⟩ _____

4 A farmer picked 5 oranges. The mass of each orange is given below. 20 points

450 g, 400 g, 420 g, 445 g, 435 g
What is the mean mass of the oranges?

⟨Ans.⟩ _____

Calculations Using the Mean

Review　STEP 41

● The masses of 4 oranges are shown below.

82 g　　　　85 g　　　　87 g　　　　82 g

What is the mean mass of the oranges?　　　　〈Ans.〉 _____

1 **Answer the question.**　　　　20 points

Example

The numbers below show the goals scored by a soccer team in 6 games.

$$4, \ 0, \ 1, \ 3, \ 5, \ 2$$

Find the mean number of goals the team scored per game.

$$(4 + 0 + 1 + 3 + 5 + 2) \div 6 = 2.5$$
　　└ Include the 0 score.

〈Ans.〉　　2.5 goals

$$(4 + 1 + 3 + 5 + 2) \div 5 = 3$$
Don't make this mistake.

Mean numbers can be decimal numbers, even if goals can't be.

The table below shows the number of students absent each day for a week.
What was the mean number of absent students per day?

Number of Absent Students

Day	Mon	Tue	Wed	Thu	Fri
Number of absent students	2	1	3	0	2

$$(\boxed{} + \boxed{} + \boxed{} + 0 + \boxed{}) \div 5 = \boxed{}$$

〈Ans.〉 _____

2 **Answer the following questions.**

20 points per question

Example

Nathaniel squeezed juice from 20 oranges. The mean amount of juice per orange was 70 milliliters. How much juice did Nathaniel get in total?

$70 \times 20 = 1,400$

⟨Ans.⟩ _____1,400 mL_____

(1) Anna ran a mean distance of 3 kilometers every day for 20 days. How far did she run in total?

$3 \times \boxed{} = \boxed{}$

⟨Ans.⟩ _____

(2) The mean number of daily absences in Jasmine's class during November was 0.7. There were 20 school days in November. How many total absences were there in the month?

⟨Ans.⟩ _____

(3) Fran walked from home to school in 580 steps. The mean length of one step was 0.6 meters. How far is it from Fran's home to her school? Round your answer to the nearest 10 meters.

⟨Ans.⟩ _____

(4) The table shows the number of books the students in Toby's class borrowed from the school library each day for one week. Supposing that this week represents a typical week, estimate how many books students in Toby's class will borrow over 20 days.

Number of Books Borrowed

Day	Mon	Tue	Wed	Thu	Fri
Number of books borrowed	6	5	7	0	8

⟨Ans.⟩ _____

Review STEP 42

- Imani picked 4 tomatoes from her garden. The mass of each tomato in grams (g) is below.

  257 g, 261 g, 259 g, 263 g

  Use this information to estimate the total mass of 20 tomatoes from her garden. Provide your answer in kilograms (kg).

  ⟨Ans.⟩ _____

1 **Answer the question below.**   10 points

Example

Two groups of people, A and B, picked up cans littering the beach.

Picking Up Cans

Group	Number of people	Mean number of cans per person
A	18	15
B	12	10

Find the mean number of cans per person for groups A and B combined.

Total number of cans $15 \times 18 + 10 \times 12 = 390$

Total number of people $18 + 12 = 30$

Mean number of cans per person in groups A and B $390 \div 30 = 13$

⟨Ans.⟩   13 cans

Two groups, A and B, competed in a long jump contest.

Long-Jump Results

Group	Number of people	Mean distance per person (cm)
A	14	265
B	16	268

What is the mean distance, for both groups combined?
Round your answer to the nearest whole number.   ⟨Ans.⟩ _____

2 **Alice has taken 3 math tests this year. Her mean test score is 75. She is about to take another math test. Answer the questions below based on this information.**

15 points per question

(1) What is the sum of Alice's 3 test scores so far?

$$\boxed{} \times 3 = \boxed{}$$

⟨Ans.⟩ _____

(2) If she gets 95 points on her 4ᵗʰ test, what will the new sum of her scores be?

$$\boxed{} + 95 = \boxed{}$$

⟨Ans.⟩ _____

(3) If she gets 95 points on her 4ᵗʰ test, what will her new mean test score be?

$$\boxed{} \div 4 = \boxed{}$$

⟨Ans.⟩ _____

3 **Simon has taken 4 English tests this year. His mean score is 88. He is about to take another English test. Answer the questions below based on this information.**

15 points per question

(1) What is the sum of Simon's scores from the first 4 tests?

⟨Ans.⟩ _____

(2) Simon hopes his 5ᵗʰ test will bring his mean score up to 90. In that case, what would be the sum of his 5 test scores?

⟨Ans.⟩ _____

(3) What score does Simon need on his 5ᵗʰ test to bring his mean test score up to 90?

⟨Ans.⟩ _____

Introduction to Spread

Date   /   /

Score

/100

Review STEP 43

- The mean height of Andrew, Beth, Catherine, and David is 138.5 centimeters. Ellen is 135.5 centimeters tall. What is the mean height for the group of 5 people?

⟨Ans.⟩ _____

1 **A farmer recorded the mass of each egg collected from two chickens, A and B. The mass of each egg in grams (g) is given in the tables below. Use the tables to answer the questions.**

15 points per question

Chicken A's Eggs (g)

① 48	② 53	③ 63	④ 58	⑤ 65	⑥ 53	⑦ 58	⑧ 56
⑨ 57	⑩ 58	⑪ 55	⑫ 60	⑬ 50	⑭ 67	⑮ 57	⑯ 62

Chicken B's Eggs (g)

① 63	② 50	③ 74	④ 54	⑤ 45	⑥ 63	⑦ 67	⑧ 54
⑨ 47	⑩ 60	⑪ 52	⑫ 57	⑬ 68			

For each chicken, calculate the mean mass of the eggs. (You can use a calculator.)

(1) Mean mass of chicken A's eggs

⟨Ans.⟩ _____

(2) Mean mass of chicken B's eggs

⟨Ans.⟩ _____

2 Use the tables on the previous page to answer the following questions.

(1) Complete the number lines below to show the mass of each egg. Some of the values are already filled in for you.   10 points per number line

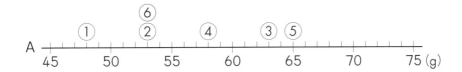

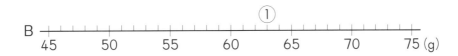

(2) For each chicken, what is the difference in mass between the most massive and least massive egg?
10 points per ☐

Chicken A ☐ g   Chicken B ☐ g

(3) Draw a ↑ on each number line to show the mean mass of eggs from each chicken. (Refer to your answers to (1) and (2) on the previous page.)   10 points per number line

(4) Judging from the number lines above, which eggs (those from chicken A or those from chicken B) tend to be farther from the mean mass of the group?   10 points

〈Ans.〉 _____

101

STEP **45**

Analyzing Data

Spread

Date   /   /

Score

/100

Review STEP 44

- The tables below show the mass in grams (g) of potatoes harvested from two fields.

Field 1 Potatoes (g)

① 264	② 276	③ 287	④ 302
⑤ 318	⑥ 268	⑦ 279	⑧ 269

Field 2 Potatoes (g)

① 240	② 263	③ 336	④ 301
⑤ 312	⑥ 286	⑦ 275	

What is the difference in mass between the most and least massive potato in field 1? How about for field 2?

Field 1 [   ] g   Field 2 [   ] g

Don't Forget!

A table of data can help you see information about the data that might not be clear from the mean.

1 **The tables below show the mass of each egg collected from two chickens, A and B. Use the tables to answer the questions on the next page.**

Chicken A's Eggs (g)

① 48	② 53	③ 63	④ 58	⑤ 65	⑥ 53	⑦ 58	⑧ 56
⑨ 57	⑩ 58	⑪ 55	⑫ 60	⑬ 50	⑭ 67	⑮ 57	⑯ 62

Chicken B's Eggs (g)

① 63	② 50	③ 74	④ 54	⑤ 45	⑥ 63	⑦ 67	⑧ 54
⑨ 47	⑩ 60	⑪ 52	⑫ 57	⑬ 68			

(1) Fill in the tables below using the information from the previous page.   25 points per table

Chicken A's Eggs

Mass range (g)	Number of eggs
45 to 49.99	1
50 to 54.99	3
55 to 59.99	
60 to 64.99	
65 to 69.99	
70 to 74.99	
Total	

Chicken B's Eggs

Mass range (g)	Number of eggs
45 to 49.99	
50 to 54.99	
55 to 59.99	
60 to 64.99	
65 to 69.99	
70 to 74.99	
Total	

(2) How many eggs from each chicken have a mass of less than 50 grams?   10 points per ☐

A ☐   B ☐

(3) For each chicken, what percentage of eggs have a mass of at least 65 grams? Round your answer to the nearest whole number.   10 points per question

A

⟨Ans.⟩ about _____

B

⟨Ans.⟩ about _____

(4) Think about the egg from chicken A with the 5th lowest mass. Which mass range is this egg in?   10 points

⟨Ans.⟩ _____

Introduction to Histograms

Date / /

Score /100

Review STEP 45

- The table to the right shows the mass of each egg collected from Chicken C. What percentage of eggs have a mass between 55 and 64.99 grams? Round your answer to the nearest whole number.

⟨Ans.⟩ _____

Eggs from Chicken C

Mass range (g)	Number of eggs
45 to 49.99	2
50 to 54.99	4
55 to 59.99	1
60 to 64.99	3
65 to 69.99	2
70 to 74.99	1
Total	13

Don't Forget! Histograms

The graph below is called a **histogram**. It uses data from the table on the right. Histograms are useful for summarizing and identifying key features of data.

Eggs from Chicken D

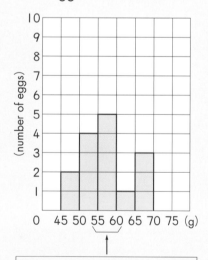

The histogram shows that there are 5 eggs in this mass range.

Eggs from Chicken D

Mass range (g)	Number of eggs
45 to 49.99	2
50 to 54.99	4
55 to 59.99	5
60 to 64.99	1
65 to 69.99	3
70 to 74.99	0
Total	15

STEP 1-2
Rounding

STEP 3-6
Introduction to Ratios

STEP 7-15
Percentages

STEP 16-24
Unit Rates

STEP 25-40
Ratios and Proportions

STEP 41-47
Analyzing Data

STEP 48-53
Number of Possible Outcomes

1 The histogram on the right shows the height in meters (m) of trees in a section of forest.

20 points per question

(1) Which height range includes the most trees?

⟨Ans.⟩ _____

(2) How many trees are 35 to 40 meters tall?

⟨Ans.⟩ _____

(3) What percentage of trees are at least 50 meters tall?

⟨Ans.⟩ _____

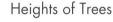
Heights of Trees

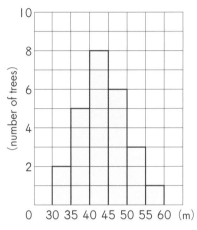

2 The histograms below show how far in meters each player on Team 1 and Team 2 threw a softball.

20 points per question

Team 1 Softball Throwing Distances

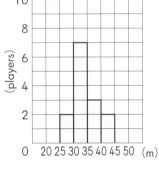

Team 2 Softball Throwing Distances

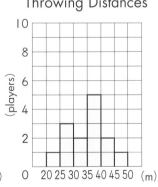

(1) Which team had more players throw at least 40 meters?

⟨Ans.⟩ _____

(2) Which team had a greater difference between the shortest distance thrown and the longest distance thrown?

⟨Ans.⟩ _____

105

Analyzing Data

Drawing Histograms

Date / /

Score /100

Review STEP 46

- The histogram on the right shows the heights in centimeters (cm) of students in the school choir. How many students are shorter than 145 centimeters?

⟨Ans.⟩ _____

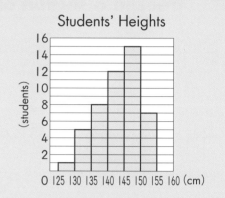

Students' Heights

Don't Forget! How to Make a Histogram

You can use the following steps to present data in a histogram.

Students' Travel Time to School (min)

9	13	7	8	20	12	6	13	18	8
10	4	14	13	9	11	23	26	7	3
9	14	2	5						

Organize the data into groups—in this case, time range.

Students' Travel Time to School

Time range (min)	Number of students
0 to 4.99	3
5 to 9.99	9
10 to 14.99	8
15 to 19.99	1
20 to 24.99	2
25 to 29.99	1

Use the organized data to make a histogram.

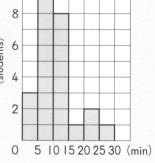

Students' Travel Time to School

1 The table below shows softball throwing distances for students in a class. Answer the following questions.

20 points per question

Softball Throwing Distances (m)

① 14	② 10	③ 16	④ 17	⑤ 13	⑥ 9	⑦ 21	⑧ 18
⑨ 23	⑩ 24	⑪ 19	⑫ 27	⑬ 26	⑭ 13	⑮ 31	⑯ 29
⑰ 8	⑱ 14	⑲ 25	⑳ 23	㉑ 28	㉒ 26	㉓ 22	

(1) Calculate the mean. Round your answer to the nearest whole number.
(You can use a calculator.)

〈Ans.〉 about _____

(2) Fill in the table of distance ranges on the bottom left of the page.

(3) Which distance range includes the most students?

〈Ans.〉 _____

What percentage of students are in this distance range?

〈Ans.〉 about _____

(4) Make a histogram based on the table.

Distance range (m)	Students
5 to 9.99	
10 to 14.99	
15 to 19.99	
20 to 24.99	
25 to 29.99	
30 to 34.99	
Total	

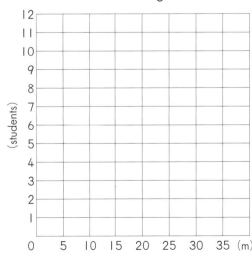

Softball Throwing Distances

107

Introduction to Permutations

Review STEP 47

● For each item below, indicate whether the information can be found using <u>only</u> the histogram on the right. Write "yes" or "no."

(1) The number of rocks with a mass from 50 up to 55 grams.

⟨Ans.⟩ _____

(2) The number of rocks that have a mass of 50 grams.

⟨Ans.⟩ _____

(3) The number of rocks that have a mass of less than 55 grams.

⟨Ans.⟩ _____

Rocks Collected

(number of rocks)

0 45 50 55 60 65 70 75 (g)

1 Answer the following question.

30 points

Example

Find the number of ways Ali (A), Beth (B), and Chris (C) can line up in a row.

①	②	③
A	B	C
A	C	B
B	A	C
B	C	A
C	A	B
C	B	A

When Ali is in front (2 ways)

When Bob is in front (2 ways)

When Chris is in front (2 ways)

There are 6 ways in total.

Robin makes 3-digit numbers by using these cards: ☐1☐, ☐2☐, ☐3☐.
Write down all the possible numbers she can make.

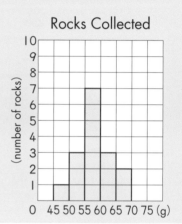

1	2	3
1	3	2
2		
2		
3		
3		

⟨Ans.⟩ 123, 132,

2 Alex (A), Bess (B), Christina (C), and David (D) are doing relay practice. Write down all the possible variations of the order. 35 points

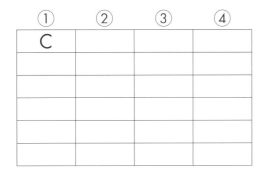

①	②	③	④
A	B	C	D
A	B	D	C
A	C	B	
A	C		
A	D		
A			

①	②	③	④
B			
B			
B			
B			
B			
B			

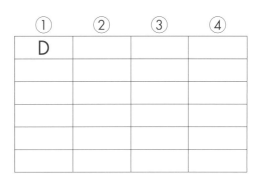

①	②	③	④
C			

①	②	③	④
D			

3 Ann (A), Brie (B), Cole (C), and Danny (D) are taking turns reading aloud. How many possible orders are there for taking turns? Complete the figures, and then write your answer. 35 points

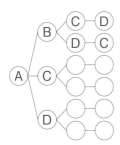
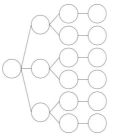
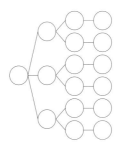

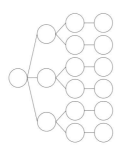

⟨Ans.⟩ _____

Review STEP 48

- May wants to hang up 3 flags in a row: a red flag, a blue flag, and a yellow flag. In how many different ways can she order the 3 flags?

⟨Ans.⟩ _____

1 **Answer the following question.** 20 points

Example

Julie makes 2-digit numbers by using 2 of these 3 number cards: ⬚1⬚, ⬚2⬚, ⬚3⬚. There are 6 numbers she can make.

| 1 2 | | 1 3 | | 2 1 | | 2 3 | | 3 1 | | 3 2 |

Keisha makes 2-digit numbers by using 2 of these 4 number cards: ⬚1⬚, ⬚2⬚, ⬚3⬚, ⬚4⬚. Write out all the numbers she can make.

| 1 2 | | 2 1 | | 3 ⬚ | | ⬚ ⬚ |

| 1 3 | | 2 3 | | ⬚ ⬚ | | ⬚ ⬚ |

| 1 4 | | 2 4 | | ⬚ ⬚ | | ⬚ ⬚ |

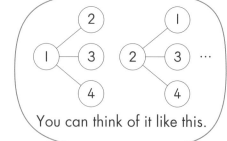

You can think of it like this.

2 There are 4 number cards: ⌐0⌐, ⌐1⌐, ⌐2⌐, ⌐3⌐. Elizabeth makes numbers to one decimal place by using 2 of these cards and putting a decimal point between them. However, she doesn't make whole numbers, such as 1.0, 2.0, and 3.0.

20 points per question

(1) Write down all the possible numbers Elizabeth can make that are smaller than 1.

0.1

(2) Write down all the possible numbers Elizabeth can make that are smaller than 3.

3 There are 4 number cards: ⌐3⌐, ⌐4⌐, ⌐5⌐, ⌐6⌐. Mark makes fractions by using 2 of these cards, one as the numerator and the other as the denominator.

20 points per question

(1) Write down all the possible fractions Mark can make that are smaller than 1.

(2) Write down all the possible fractions Mark can make that are bigger than 1.

Different Types of Sample Spaces

Date   /   /

Score   /100

Review STEP 49

- Anthony (A), Brandy (B), Charles (C), and Daniella (D) each want to be president or vice president of the debate team. Write down all the possible options. (Suppose the first letter in each pair represents the president and the second letter represents the vice president.)

---

1   **Answer the following question.**   20 points

Example

You plan to flip a coin twice in a row. Write down all the possible outcomes of heads (H) and tails (T). How many different outcomes are there?

①	②
H	H
H	T
T	H
T	T

⟨Ans.⟩   4 outcomes

You plan to flip a coin three times in a row. Write down all the possible outcomes of heads and tails.

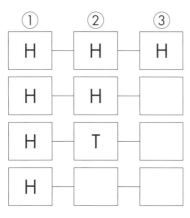

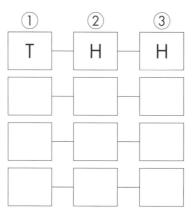

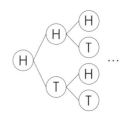

This is another way to show the outcomes.

2 Julian and Lee will play a round of "rock, paper, scissors."

15 points per question

(1) In this game, each player picks rock (R), paper (P), or scissors (S). Write down the possible outcomes for Julian and Lee's choices. (Suppose the first letter in each pair represents Julian's choice, and the second letter represents Lee's choice.)

R-R,

(2) How many ways can Julian win? (In "rock, paper, scissors," rock beats scissors, scissors beats paper, and paper beats rock.)

⟨Ans.⟩ _____

3 Christina has two 6-sided dice. She rolls one, and then the next, and adds the values of the top faces. How many ways are there to get a total of 7? (Assume that the order in which the numbers are rolled does matter.) Write them all out.

25 points

⟨Ans.⟩ _____

4 Study the grid below. How many routes can you trace from point A to point I by moving only upward or right along the gridlines?

25 points

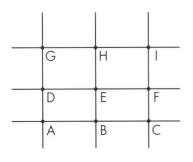

⟨Ans.⟩ _____

Review STEP 50

● You plan to flip a coin 3 times in a row. How many possible combinations of heads and tails are there?

⟨Ans.⟩ _____

1 **Answer the following question.**

30 points

Example

Soccer teams A, B, and C will all play against each other one time. How many games will there be?

	A	B	C
A		✓	✓
B	✓		✓
C	✓	✓	

Each cell in the table represents a possible combination. A team cannot play itself, so those cells are crossed out.

A – B   B~A
A – C   C~A
B – C   C~B

Look at all the combinations. The order of the team names does not matter, so A–B and B–A describe the same game. Remove these duplicates.

⟨Ans.⟩   **3 games**

Baseball teams A, B, C, and D will all play each other once. How many games will there be? Write down all of them.

	A	B	C	D
A				
B				
C				
D				

⟨Ans.⟩ _____

2 **Soccer teams A, B, C, D, and E will all play each other once. How many games will there be? Write down all of them.** 35 points

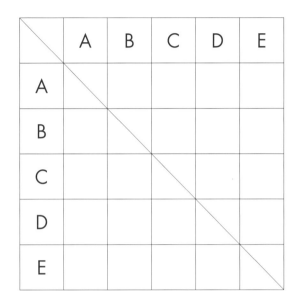

⟨Ans.⟩ _____

3 **Tennis players Angie (A), Bart (B), Charlotte (C), Denise (D), Eduardo (E), and Frank (F) will all play each other once. How many tennis matches will there be? Write down all of them.**

35 points

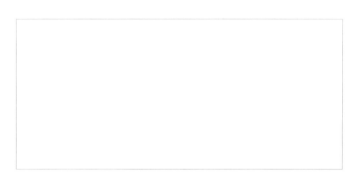

⟨Ans.⟩ _____

Number of Possible Outcomes
Combinations

Review STEP 51

● Basketball teams A, B, C, and D will all play each other once. How many games will there be?

〈Ans.〉 _____

1 **Answer the following question.**

20 points for completion

Example

Crystal can play 5 notes on her instrument: A, B, C, D, and E. How many different combinations of 2 notes can she play? (The order of the notes does not matter.) Write down all of them.

(A , B)   (B , C)   (C , D)   (D , E)
(A , C)   (B , D)   (C , E)
(A , D)   (B , E)
(A , E)

〈Ans.〉 10 combinations

There are 5 people: Allie (A), Bella (B), Charles (C), Dan (D), and Emma (E). Of these 5 people, 3 will become members of a committee. How many different combinations of 3 people can be made from these 5? (Order does not matter.) Write down all of them.

(A , B , C)   (B , C , D)   (,   ,)
(A , B , D)   (,   ,)
(,   ,)   (,   ,)
(,   ,)
(,   ,)
(,   ,)

〈Ans.〉 _____

2 Axel (A), Bob (B), Chloe (C), and Dion (D) do the cleaning in pairs.

20 points per question

（1） Write down all the possible pair combinations.

（2） How many combinations are there?

⟨Ans.⟩ _____

3 Eva has 4 types of flowers: A, B, C, and D. She will choose 3 types and put them together in a vase. (Order does not matter.)

20 points per question

（1） Write down all the possible combinations.

（2） How many combinations are there?

⟨Ans.⟩ _____

Applying Combinations

Review STEP 52

● Greg has 4 types of snacks available: A, B, C, and D. He will choose 2 of them. How many different combinations can he make?

⟨Ans.⟩ _____

1 **Answer the following question.** 25 points

Example

There are 4 small weights beside a scale: 1 gram, 10 grams, 50 grams, and 100 grams. If Amir picks up 2 of the 4 weights, what are all the possible combinations? What is the total mass of each of those combinations?

(1 gram, 10 grams)   (10 grams, 50 grams)   (50 grams, 100 grams)
(1 gram, 50 grams)   (10 grams, 100 grams)
(1 gram, 100 grams)

⟨Ans.⟩ 11 g, 51 g, 101 g, 60 g, 110 g, 150 g

There are 4 small weights beside a scale: 10 grams, 50 grams, 100 grams, and 500 grams. If Evan picks up 2 of the 4 weights, what is the total mass of each possible combination?

2 There are 4 weights: 1 gram, 5 grams, 10 grams, and 50 grams. If Rachel picks up 2 of the 4 weights, what is the total mass of each possible combination?

25 points

3 There are 4 weights: 1 gram, 5 grams, 10 grams, and 50 grams. If Rick picks up 3 of the 4 weights, what is the total mass of each possible combination?

25 points

4 There are 4 weights: two 500-gram weights and two 100-gram weights. Write down the total mass of each possible combination you could form by picking up some or all of the weights, from 1 weight to all 4.

25 points

Analyzing Data and Number of Possible Outcomes

Date / /

Score

/100

Review STEP 41 – STEP 45 · **The tables below show the mass, in grams (g), of each sweet potato grown in gardens A and B.**

12 points

Garden A's Sweet Potatoes (g)

265	278	287	308
268	319	269	

Garden B's Sweet Potatoes (g)

261	280	302	287
275	310	284	269

Which garden produced the more massive sweet potatoes, based on mean mass?

⟨Ans.⟩

Review STEP 46 STEP 47 · **The histogram on the right shows the mass of each plum picked today.**

14 points per question

(1) How many plums were picked?

⟨Ans.⟩

(2) Of the total number of plums picked, what percentage have a mass in the range from 60 up to 65 grams? Round your answer to the nearest whole number.

⟨Ans.⟩ about

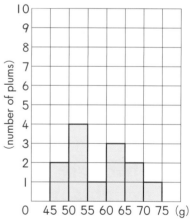

Plums Picked Today

(number of plums)

Review STEP 48 · **Ashley (A), Bruce (B), Carol (C), and Dylan (D) are about to a run a relay race. Only 1 person will run at a time, and all 4 will run. How many possible variations of the order of runners are there?**

12 points

⟨Ans.⟩

Review STEP **49** Julian makes 2-digit numbers by using 2 of these 4 number cards: ⬜1, ⬜2, ⬜3, ⬜4. How many different numbers can he make?

12 points

⟨Ans.⟩ _____

Review STEP **50** You plan to flip a coin 3 times in a row. How many possible outcomes of heads and tails are there?

12 points

⟨Ans.⟩ _____

Review STEP **51** Soccer teams A, B, C, D, and E will all play each other once. How many games will there be?

12 points

⟨Ans.⟩ _____

Review STEP **52** STEP **53** There are 3 small weights: 1 gram, 2 grams, and 4 grams. Write down the total mass of each possible combination you could form by picking up some or all of the weights, from 1 weight to all 3.

12 points

Challenge

1 After a car travels 180 kilometers, it has 24 liters of gasoline left. The car travels another 45 kilometers and has 19 liters of gasoline left. How much gasoline was in this car at the start?

13 points

⟨Ans.⟩ _____

2 The chart below shows the ratio of nutrients in a piece of food.

13 points per question

Water	Protein	Fat	⊢ Other

0   10   20   30   40   50   60   70   80   90   100%

(1) What percentage of the food is protein?

⟨Ans.⟩ _____

(2) If this food has a mass of 40 grams, how many grams of fat does it contain?

⟨Ans.⟩ _____

3 The mass of 1,000 sheets of a certain kind of paper is 1.5 kilograms. If you have 3.9 kilograms of this kind of paper, how many sheets do you have?

12 points

⟨Ans.⟩ _____

4 x is inversely proportional to y. When x is 12, y is 21. When y is 28, what is the value of x?

12 points

⟨Ans.⟩ _____

5 There are five cards: 0, 1, 2, 3, and 4. When Simon lines up all the cards and makes 5-digit numbers, how many odd numbers (whole numbers that cannot be evenly divided by 2) can he make?

12 points

⟨Ans.⟩ _____

6 The table and histogram below show the heights in centimeters (cm) of the 6th graders at Emma's school. The table shows the data for class 6-A, and the histogram shows the data for class 6-B. Emma is in class 6-B, and her height is 151.5 centimeters. If all the students from the two classes line up in order of increasing height, where might Emma be in the line? Your answer should be a range of numbers.

12 points

Class 6-A

Height range (cm)	Number of people
125 to 129.99	2
130 to 134.99	4
135 to 139.99	7
140 to 144.99	11
145 to 149.99	7
150 to 154.99	4
155 to 159.99	5

Class 6-B

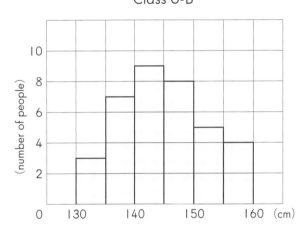

⟨Ans.⟩ between _____ and _____

7 The average score of Alex, Brad, Chris, David, and Elizabeth is 2 points lower than the average score of just Chris, David, and Elizabeth. The total score of Alex and Brad is 160. What is the average score of all 5 people?

13 points

⟨Ans.⟩ _____

Math Boosters Grades 4-6 Problem Solving with Ratios & Proportions

Answer Key

STEP 1 (P.4 · 5)

1 (1) 3,000 (2) 7,000
(3) 4,000 (4) 5,000
(5) 50,000 (6) 63,000
(7) 64,000 (8) 100,000

2 (1) 60,000 (2) 70,000
(3) 20,000 (4) 90,000
(5) 180,000 (6) 230,000
(7) 860,000 (8) 1,740,000

3 (1) 1,500,000 (2) 2,700,000
(3) 500,000 (4) 5,200,000
(5) 7,800,000 (6) 1,000,000
(7) 900,000

STEP 2 (P.6 · 7)

■ **Review of Step 1**
(1) 250,000
(2) 800,000

1 (1) $400 + 100 = 500$
(2) $600 - 300 = 300$
(3) $2,100 + 300 = 2,400$
(4) $7,700 - 1,000 = 6,700$
(5) $300 + 300 + 1,800 = 2,400$

2 (1) $600 \times 400 = 240,000$
(2) $600 \div 200 = 3$
(3) $500 \times 300 = 150,000$
(4) $39,300 \div 300 = 131$
(5) $400 \times 4,400 = 1,760,000$
(6) $4,000 \div 2,000 = 2$

3 (1) c (2) b (3) d

STEP 3 (P.8 · 9)

■ **Review of Step 2**
(1) $3,100 + 500 = 3,600$
(2) $600 \times 200 = 120,000$

1 (1) $20 \div 5 = 4$
(2) $55 \div 11 = 5$
(3) $180 \div 4 = 45$

2 (1) $50 \div 20 = 2.5$
(2) $30 \div 20 = 1.5$
(3) $46 \div 20 = 2.3$
(4) $130 \div 50 = 2.6$
(5) $2,800 \div 800 = 3.5$
(6) $1,800 \div 1,500 = 1.2$
(7) $11,250 \div 2,500 = 4.5$

STEP 4 (P.10 · 11)

■ **Review of Step 3**
(1) $30 \div 10 = 3$
(2) $5,400 \div 1,200 = 4.5$

1 (1) $12 \div 2 = 6$ Ans. 6 m
(2) $60 \div 3 = 20$ Ans. 20 m

2 (1) $12 \div 1.5 = 8$ Ans. 8 m
(2) $2,800 \div 3.5 = 800$ Ans. 800 dollars
(3) $630 \div 1.8 = 350$ Ans. 350 g
(4) $13.8 \div 0.6 = 23$ Ans. 23 km²
(5) $124.5 \div 0.15 = 830$ Ans. 830 kg

STEP 5 (P.12 · 13)

■ **Review of Step 4**
$12.5 \div 0.5 = 25$ Ans. 25 g

1 (1) $6 \div 10 = 0.6$ Ans. 0.6 times
(2) $14 \div 20 = 0.7$ Ans. 0.7 times
(3) $3 \div 15 = 0.2$ Ans. 0.2 times

②
(1) $7 \div 10 = 0.7$ Ans. 0.7
(2) $3 \div 5 = 0.6$ Ans. 0.6
(3) $2 \div 5 = 0.4$ Ans. 0.4
(4) $7 \div 7 = 1$ Ans. 1
(5) $0 \div 5 = 0$ Ans. 0

STEP 6   (P.14・15)

■ **Review of Step 5**
$8 \div 10 = 0.8$ Ans. 0.8

①
(1) Ratio of boys to total: $7 \div 10 = 0.7$
     Ratio of girls to total: $3 \div 10 = 0.3$
(2) Ratio of boys to total: $1 \div 4 = 0.25$
     Ratio of girls to total: $3 \div 4 = 0.75$
(3) Ratio of boys to total: $6 \div 15 = 0.4$
     Ratio of girls to total: $9 \div 15 = 0.6$

② $128 \div 800 = 0.16$ Ans. 0.16

③
(1) $9 \div 20 = 0.45$ Ans. 0.45
(2) $11 \div 20 = 0.55$ Ans. 0.55

④
(1) $24 \div 30 = 0.8$ Ans. 0.8
(2) $35 \div 20 = 1.75$ Ans. 1.75

STEP 7   (P.16・17)

■ **Review of Step 6**
$18 \div 30 = 0.6$ Ans. 0.6

①
(1) 4 %   (2) 16 %
(3) 9 %   (4) 45 %
(5) 40 %   (6) 100 %
(7) 108 %   (8) 200 %
(9) 0.5 %   (10) 80.6 %

②
(1) 0.03   (2) 0.07
(3) 0.14   (4) 0.6
(5) 0.98   (6) 1
(7) 2.5   (8) 3.07
(9) 0.008   (10) 0.502

③
(1) $7 \div 10 = 0.7$ Ans. 70 %
(2) $15 \div 25 = 0.6$ Ans. 60 %
(3) $42 \div 30 = 1.4$ Ans. 140 %

STEP 8   (P.18・19)

■ **Review of Step 7**
(1) 29 %   (2) 60 %

①
(1) $3 \div 100 = 0.03$ Ans. 3 %
(2) $120 \div 150 = 0.8$ Ans. 80 %

② $520 \div 650 = 0.8$ Ans. 80 %

③ $50 \div 400 = 0.125$ Ans. 12.5 %

④ $360 \div 2,400 = 0.15$ Ans. 15 %

⑤ $321 \div 6,420 = 0.05$ Ans. 5 %

STEP 9   (P.20・21)

■ **Review of Step 8**
$160 \div 200 = 0.8$ Ans. 80%

①
(1) 0.2
     $500 \times 0.2 = 100$ Ans. 100 notebooks
(2) $75 \times 1.2 = 90$ Ans. 90 tickets

②
(1) $100 \times 0.3 = 30$ Ans. 30 g
(2) $150 \times 0.3 = 45$ Ans. 45 mL
(3) $700 \times 0.85 = 595$ Ans. 595 dollars
(4) $48 \times 0.25 = 12$ Ans. 12 people
(5) $300 \times 1.5 = 450$ Ans. 450 people

③ $320 \times 0.85 = 272$ Ans. 272 g

STEP 10   (P.22・23)

■ **Review of Step 9**
$120 \times 0.7 = 84$ Ans. 84 people

① $1 - 0.25 = 0.75$
       $500 \times 0.75 = 375$ Ans. 375 dollars

② $1 + 0.05 = 1.05$
$800 \times 1.05 = 840$ Ans. 840 dollars

③ $1 - 0.2 = 1.2$
$1,500 \times 1.2 = 1,800$ Ans. 1,800 kg

④ $1 - 0.06 = 0.94$
$450 \times 0.94 = 423$ Ans. 423 students

STEP 11   (P.24 · 25)

■ Review of Step 10
$700 \times 0.85 = 595$ Ans. 595 dollars

❶ $400 \times 0.25 = 100$
$400 - 100 = 300$ Ans. 300 dollars

❷ $200 \times 0.05 = 10$
$200 + 10 = 210$ Ans. 210 dollars

❸ $2,800 \times 0.3 = 840$
$2,800 + 840 = 3,640$ Ans. 3,640 kg

❹ $550 \times 0.08 = 44$
$550 - 44 = 506$ Ans. 506 students

STEP 12   (P.26 · 27)

■ Review of Step 11
$300 \times 0.08 = 24$
$300 + 24 = 324$ Ans. 324 dollars

❶ $1 + 0.3 = 1.3$
$156 \div 1.3 = 120$ Ans. 120 g

❷ $1 + 0.2 = 1.2$
$90 \div 1.2 = 75$ Ans. 75 seats

❸ $84 \div 0.35 = 240$ Ans. 240 m²

❹ $(1 - 0.2 = 0.8)$
$560 \div 0.8 = 700$ Ans. 700 dollars

❺ $(1 - 0.08 = 0.92)$
$230 \div 0.92 = 250$ Ans. 250 donuts

STEP 13   (P.28 · 29)

■ Review of Step 12
$1 - 0.2 = 0.8$ $120 \div 0.8 = 150$ Ans. 150 dollars

❶ (1) 65 %
(2) 20 %
(3) 10 %

❷ (1) 48 %
(2) 21 %
(3) about $\frac{1}{5}$
(4) 3 times

❸ (1) 45 %
(2) 29 %
(3) about $\frac{1}{5}$
(4) about 3 times

STEP 14   (P.30 · 31)

■ Review of Step 13
(1) 20 %   (2) about $\frac{1}{3}$

❶ (1) West: $12 \div 40 \times 100 = 30$ (%)
North: $6 \div 40 \times 100 = 15$ (%)
South: $4 \div 40 \times 100 = 10$ (%)
(2) 100 %
(3)

Student Population by Region		
Region	Students	Percentage (%)
East	18	45
West	12	(30)
North	6	(15)
South	4	(10)
Total	40	(100)

❷ (1) Playground: $18 \div 40 \times 100 = 45$ (%)
Gym: $15 \div 40 \times 100 = 38$ (%)
Hallway: $4 \div 40 \times 100 = 10$ (%)
Classroom: $3 \div 40 \times 100 = 8$ (%)
(2) 101 %
(3) The percentage for playground could be 44 %.

(4)

Injuries by Location		
Location	Number of injuries	Percentage (%)
Playground	18	(44)
Gym	15	(38)
Hallway	4	(10)
Classroom	3	(8)
Total	40	(100)

STEP 15

(P.32・33)

■ Review of Step 14

Number of Drinks Ordered		
Drink	Number of orders	Percentage (%)
Coffee	29	(37)
Tea	21	26
Juice	17	(21)
Water	13	16
Total	80	(100)

1 Number of Cans Collected

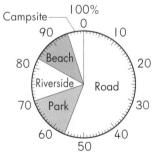

2 (1)

Types of Books in the Library		
Type	Books	Percentage (%)
Fiction	46	(38)
Science	36	(30)
History	26	(22)
Other	12	(10)
Total	120	(100)

(2) Types of Books in the Library

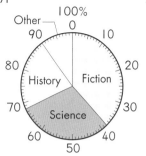

3 (1)

Types of Stores		
Type	Stores	Percentage (%)
Supermarket	29	(33)
Electronics store	22	(24)
Clothing store	17	(19)
Flower store	3	(3)
Other	19	(21)
Total	90	(100)

(2) Types of Stores

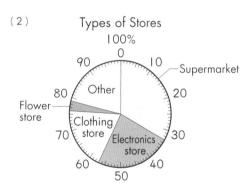

TEST

(P.34・35)

Review of Step 1

(1) the lowest number: 75
the highest number: 84
(2) the lowest number: 345
the highest number: 354

Review of Step 2

(1) $300 + 100 = 400$ Ans. 400
(2) $8,400 - 1,700 = 6,700$ Ans. 6,700
(3) $500 \times 300 = 150,000$ Ans. 150,000
(4) $4,600 \div 200 = 23$ Ans. 23

Review of Steps 3,4

(1) $30 \div 1.5 = 20$ Ans. 20 m

(2) $27.6 \div 0.6 = 46$ Ans. 46 km²

Review of Steps 5,6

$5 \div 50 = 0.1$ Ans. 0.1

Review of Steps 7,8

(1) 4 %   (2) 0.6 %

Review of Steps 9-12

$75 \times 1.4 = 105$ Ans. 105 tickets

Review of Steps 13-15

(1) 55 %

(2) $\dfrac{1}{3}$

STEP 16 (P.36 · 37)

■ **Review of Step 15**

Total Industrial Output

❶ (1) B

(2) Chicken coop A

$8 \div 4 = 2$ Ans. 2 chickens

Chicken coop B

$10 \div 4 = 2.5$ Ans. 2.5 chickens

❷ (1) A

(2) C

(3) Rabbit hutch A

$9 \div 6 = 1.5$ Ans. 1.5 rabbits

Rabbit hutch C

$8 \div 5 = 1.6$ Ans. 1.6 rabbits

Rabbit hutch D

$15 \div 9 = 1.66... \rightarrow 1.7$ Ans. 1.7 rabbits

(4) more

(5) D

(6) Rabbit hutch A

$6 \div 9 = 0.666... \rightarrow 0.67$ Ans. 0.67 m²

Rabbit hutch C

$5 \div 8 = 0.625 \rightarrow 0.63$ Ans. 0.63 m²

STEP 17 (P.38 · 39)

■ **Review of Step 16**

pool B

❶ (1) City A

$1,810,000 \div 7,406 = 244.3...$

Ans. 244 people/km²

City B

$1,440,000 \div 5,678 = 253.6...$

Ans. 254 people/km²

(2) city B

❷ (1) City A

$2,340,000 \div 7,286 = 321.1...$

Ans. 321 people/km²

City B

$1,400,000 \div 3,691 = 379.3...$

Ans. 379 people/km²

City C

$850,000 \div 2,440 = 348.3...$

Ans. 348 people/km²

(2) city B

(3) city A

STEP 18 (P.40 · 41)

■ **Review of Step 17**

$7,400 \div 20 = 370$ Ans. 370 people/km²

❶ (1) Field A $90 \div 15 = 6$ Ans. 6 kg/m²

Field B $124 \div 20 = 6.2$ Ans. 6.2 kg/m²

(2) field B

❷ 91 dollars for 7 books $91 \div 7 = 13$

72 dollars for 6 books $72 \div 6 = 12$

Ans. 91 dollars for 7 books

③   Car A $108 \div 12 = 9$

      Car B $152 \div 16 = 9.5$ Ans. car B

④   Rod A $240 \div 3 = 80$

      Rod B $370 \div 5 = 74$ Ans. rod A

STEP 19 (P.42 · 43)

■ **Review of Step 18**

Yellow tape $20 \div 8 = 2.5$

White tape $13 \div 5 = 2.6$ Ans. yellow tape

❶ (1) $15 \times 32 = 480$ Ans. 480 km

   (2) $630 \div 15 = 42$ Ans. 42 L

❷ (1) $0.5 \times 8.4 = 4.2$ Ans. 4.2 kg

   (2) $1.6 \div 0.5 = 3.2$ Ans. 3.2 m²

❸ (1) Machine A

      $450 \div 5 = 90$ Ans. 90 sheets/minute

      Machine B

      $480 \div 6 = 80$ Ans. 80 sheets/minute

   (2) $90 \times 7 = 630$ Ans. 630 sheets

   (3) $1,200 \div 80 = 15$ Ans. 15 minutes

STEP 20 (P.44 · 45)

■ **Review of Step 19**

A $450 \div 15 = 30$

B $720 \div 25 = 28.8$ Ans. pump A

❶ (1) $70 \div 2 = 35$ Ans. 35 km/h

   (2) $90 \div 3 = 30$ Ans. 30 km/h

❷ (1) $1,800 \div 10 = 180$ Ans. 180 m/min

   (2) $2,400 \div 30 = 80$ Ans. 80 m/min

❸ (1) $120 \div 8 = 15$ Ans. 15 m/s

   (2) $210 \div 30 = 7$ Ans. 7 m/s

STEP 21 (P.46 · 47)

■ **Review of Step 20**

$120 \div 3 = 40$ Ans. 40 km/h

❶ (1) Ali

   (2) Caitlyn

   (3) $100 \div 20 = 5$ Ans. 5 m/s

   (4) $18 \div 80 = 0.225$ Ans. 0.225 seconds

❷   Car A $2,000 \div 10 = 200$ m/min

      Car B $1,500 \div 6 = 250$ m/min

               Ans. car B

❸   Car A $150 \div 2 = 75$ km/h

      Car B $240 \div 3 = 80$ km/h

               Ans. car B

❹   Rea $60 \div 10 = 6$ m/s

      Felix $120 \div 24 = 5$ m/s

               Ans. Rea

STEP 22 (P.48 · 49)

■ **Review of Step 21**

Car A $3,000 \div 15 = 200$ m/min

Car B $2,000 \div 8 = 250$ m/min   Ans. car B

❶ (1) $340 \times 60 = 20,400$ Ans. 20,400 m/min

   (2) $6 \times 60 = 360$ Ans. 360 m/min

   (3) $900,000 \div 60 = 15,000$

               Ans. 15,000 m/min

❷ (1) $480 \div 2 = 240$ Ans. 240 km/h

   (2) $240 \text{ km} = 240,000$ m

      1 hour $= 60$ minutes

      $240,000 \div 60 = 4,000$

               Ans. 4,000 m/min

   (3) 1 minute $= 60$ seconds

      $4,000 \div 60 = 66.6... \rightarrow 67$ Ans. 67 m/s

STEP 23 (P.50・51)

■ Review of Step 22
$216 \div 4 = 54$ km/h
$54 \times 1,000 = 54,000$ m/h
$54,000 \div 60 = 900$ m/min　　Ans. 900 m/min

① (1) $\boxed{40} \times \boxed{2} = \boxed{80}$　　Ans. 80 km
　(2) $40 \times 3 = 120$　　Ans. 120 km
　(3) $40 \times 4.5 = 180$　　Ans. 180 km

② (1) $64 \times 2 = 128$　　Ans. 128 km
　(2) $64 \times 2.5 = 160$　　Ans. 160 km

③　$10 - 7 = 3$　$12 \times 3 = 36$　　Ans. 36 km

④　$340 \times 6 \div 2 = 1,020$　　Ans. 1,020 m

STEP 24 (P.52・53)

■ Review of Step 23
$600 \times 5 = 3,000$　　$3,000$ m $= 3$ km
　　　　　　　　　　　　Ans. 3 km

① (1) $15 \div 3 = 5$　　Ans. 5 hours
　(2) $15 \div 2 = 7.5$　　Ans. 7.5 hours

② (1) 5.6 km $= 5,600$ m
　　$5,600 \div 700 = 8$　　Ans. 8 minutes
　(2) $5,600 \div 500 = 11.2$　　Ans. 11.2 minutes

③　$24,000$ m $= 24$ km
　　$24 \div 15 = 1.6$　　Ans. 1.6 hours

④ (1) $5,820 \div 60 = 97$　$97 - 60 = 37$
　　　　　　Ans. 1 minute and 37 seconds
　(2) $60 \times 60 \times 60 = 216,000$
　　$216,000$ m $= 216$ km　　Ans. 216 km/h

TEST (P.54・55)

Review of Step 16
East Park　$56 \div 140 = 0.4$
West Park　$90 \div 200 = 0.45$　　Ans. west park

Review of Step 17
$7,824 \div 38 = 205.8... \to 206$
　　　　　　　　　Ans. 206 people/km²

Review of Step 18
$80 \div 25 = 3.2$　　Ans. 3.2 kg/m²

Review of Step 19
　(1) $0.4 \times 7.2 = 2.88$　　Ans. 2.88 kg
　(2) $1.2 \div 0.4 = 3$　　Ans. 3 m²

Review of Step 20
$200 \div 2.5 = 80$　　Ans. 80 km/h

Review of Steps 21,22
$30 \times 1,000 = 30,000$
$30,000 \div 60 = 500$　　Ans. 500 m/min

Review of Step 23
$30 \times 0.5 = 15$　　Ans. 15 km

Review of Step 24
$140 \div 40 = 3.5$　　Ans. 3.5 hours

STEP 25 (P.56・57)

■ Review of Step 24
$21,600 \div 12 = 1,800$
$1,800 \div 60 = 30$　　Ans. 30 minutes

① (1) 120 base units
　(2) 60 base units
　(3) 4 base units

　© *Kumon Publishing Co., Ltd.*

2 (1) 10 base units

(2) 15 base units

(3) vinegar: 2 base units, olive oil: 3 base units

(4) 3 mL

(5) 20 mL

(6) The ratio is 2 to 3.

STEP 26
(P.58 · 59)

■ Review of Step 25
The ratio is 3 to 5.

1 (1) 5 : 9

(2) 5 : 4

(3) 25 : 16

2 (1) 8 : 17

(2) 60 : 73

(3) 4 : 15

3 (1) A : B = 2 : 3   C : D = 4 : 6

(2) C : D = 2 : 3

(3) yes

Review of Simplifying Fractions and Common Denominators
(P.60 · 61)

1 (1) $\dfrac{1}{3}$ (2) $\dfrac{3}{4}$ (3) $\dfrac{1}{2}$

(4) $\dfrac{2}{3}$ (5) $\dfrac{4}{5}$

2 (1) $\dfrac{1}{2}$ (2) $\dfrac{1}{3}$ (3) $\dfrac{3}{4}$

(4) $\dfrac{2}{5}$ (5) $\dfrac{5}{6}$

3 (1) $\dfrac{1}{2}$ (2) $\dfrac{1}{3}$ (3) $\dfrac{2}{7}$

(4) $\dfrac{1}{4}$ (5) $\dfrac{2}{3}$ (6) $\dfrac{1}{2}$

(7) $\dfrac{2}{3}$ (8) $\dfrac{2}{3}$ (9) $\dfrac{4}{5}$

4 (1) $\left(\dfrac{2}{4}, \dfrac{1}{4}\right)$ (2) $\left(\dfrac{1}{6}, \dfrac{2}{6}\right)$

(3) $\left(\dfrac{4}{12}, \dfrac{3}{12}\right)$ (4) $\left(\dfrac{8}{20}, \dfrac{15}{20}\right)$

STEP 27
(P.62 · 63)

■ Review of Step 26
A : B = 27 : 16

1 (1) $\dfrac{1}{3}$ (2) $\dfrac{2}{3}$ (3) $\dfrac{3}{4}$

(4) $\dfrac{12}{13}$ (5) $\dfrac{4}{5}$

2 (1) 2 : 6   (2) 9 : 15

(3) 15 : 6   (4) 21 : 28

STEP 28
(P.64 · 65)

■ Review of Step 27
$\dfrac{2}{3}, \dfrac{2}{3}$

1 (1)
$$1 : 2 = 2 : 4 \quad (\times \boxed{2}, \times \boxed{2})$$

(2)
$$4 : 3 = 8 : 6 \quad (\times \boxed{2}, \times \boxed{2})$$

(3)
$$5 : 2 = 15 : 6 \quad (\times \boxed{3}, \times \boxed{3})$$

2 (1) 4 : 12   (2) 1 : 3

(3) 6 : 12   (4) 1 : 2

(5) 2 : 4   (6) 36 : 72

(7) 4 : 3   (8) 80 : 60

(9) 1 : 5   (10) 20 : 100

STEP 29
(P.66 · 67)

■ Review of Step 28
15 : 6 = $\boxed{5}$: $\boxed{2}$ 5 : 4 = $\boxed{40}$: $\boxed{32}$

1 (1) 1 : 3 = 4 : $\boxed{12}$ (2) 3 : 4 = 9 : $\boxed{12}$

(3) 4 : 3 = $\boxed{16}$: 12   (4) 3 : 7 = $\boxed{9}$: 21

(5) 6 : 5 = $\boxed{36}$: 30

❷ (1) $9:12=3:\boxed{4}$　　(2) $8:12=2:\boxed{3}$

　(3) $16:12=4:\boxed{3}$　　(4) $6:8=\boxed{3}:4$

　(5) $18:12=\boxed{3}:2$　　(6) $27:18=\boxed{3}:2$

❸ (1) $4:3$　　　(2) $3:7$　　　(3) $2:7$

STEP 30

(P.68 · 69)

■ Review of Step 29
$20:15=\boxed{4}:3$　　　$12:21=4:\boxed{7}$

❶ (1) $5:6$

　(2) $8:24=1:3$

　(3) $9:12=3:4$

❷ (1) $\dfrac{5}{10}:\dfrac{6}{10}=5:6$

　(2) $\dfrac{8}{12}:\dfrac{9}{12}=8:9$

　(3) $\dfrac{15}{18}:\dfrac{4}{18}=15:4$

　(4) $\dfrac{15}{40}:\dfrac{24}{40}=15:24=5:8$

　(5) $\dfrac{12}{5}:\dfrac{30}{5}=12:30=2:5$

　(6) $\dfrac{16}{36}:\dfrac{15}{36}=16:15$

　(7) $\dfrac{21}{56}:\dfrac{20}{56}=21:20$

STEP 31

(P.70 · 71)

■ Review of Step 30
　(1) $3:5$　　　　　(2) $5:6$

❶ (Method A)　　　　　(Method B)

$5:3=\boxed{150}:x$　　　$150\times\boxed{\dfrac{3}{5}}=90$

$x=\boxed{3}\times\boxed{30}=\boxed{90}$

　　　　Ans. 90 g　　　　　Ans. 90 g

---

❷ (Method A)　　　　　　　　(Method B)

$5:8=\boxed{45}:x$　　　　$45\times\boxed{\dfrac{8}{5}}=72$

$x=\boxed{8}\times\boxed{9}=\boxed{72}$

　　　　Ans. 72 cm　　　　Ans. 72 cm

❸ (1) 25　　　(2) 3　　　(3) 2

TEST

(P.72 · 73)

Review of Step 25
　(1) 5 base units
　(2) vinegar: 1 base unit, olive oil: 3 base units

Review of Step 26
　(1) $7:16$　　　　(2) $5:17$

Review of Step 27
　　$4:6$

Review of Step 28
　(1) $4:10$　　　　(2) $2:5$

Review of Step 29
　(1) $5:25$　　　　(2) $5:4$

Review of Step 30
　(1) $5:8$　　　　(2) $5:6$

Review of Step 31
　(1) 10　　　　(2) 2

STEP 32

(P.74 · 75)

■ Review of Step 31
　(1) 5　　　　　(2) 12

❶ (1) 8, 12
　(2) It is also doubled, from 4 to 8.
　(3) It is also tripled.
　(4) yes

2 (1)

Time (min)	x	1	2	3	4	5	6	7	⋯
Volume of water (L)	y	3	6	9	12	15	18	21	⋯

Ans. yes

(2)

Parent's age	x	24	25	26	27	28	29	30	31	⋯
Child's age	y	0	1	2	3	4	5	6	7	⋯

Ans. no

(3)

Number of pieces	x	1	2	3	4	5	6	⋯
Length of each piece (cm)	y	24	12	8	6	4.8	4	⋯

Ans. no

(4)

Time traveled (h)	x	1	2	3	4	5	6	7	⋯
Distance traveled (km)	y	80	160	240	320	400	480	560	⋯

Ans. yes

(5)

Length of piece of rope (cm)	x	10	20	30	40	50	60	⋯
Mass of piece of rope (g)	y	40	80	120	160	200	240	⋯

Ans. yes

STEP 33

(P.76 · 77)

■ Review of Step 32
(1) yes   (2) no

1 (1)

Time (min.)	x	1	2	3	4	5	6	⋯
Volume of water (L)	y	4	8	12	16	20	24	⋯
$y \div x$		4	4	4	4	4	4	⋯

(2) $y \div x = 4$

(3) $y = 4 \times x$

2 (1) $y = 2 \times x$

(2) $y = 30 \times x$

3 (1) The mass per 1 meter of wire

(2) yes

(3) $y = 7 \times x$

(4) 84 g

STEP 34

(P.78 · 79)

■ Review of Step 33
$y = 5 \times x$

1 (A) x multiplied by $\dfrac{2}{5}$ y multiplied by $\dfrac{2}{5}$

(B) x multiplied by $\dfrac{2}{3}$ y multiplied by $\dfrac{2}{3}$

2 (1) yes

(2) (A) $\dfrac{1}{3}$ (B) $\dfrac{7}{5}$

(3) $y = 7 \times x$

(4) $y = 7 \times 0 = 0$ Ans. 0

   $y = 7 \times 15 = 105$ Ans. 105

(5) $x = 364 \div 7 = 52$ Ans. 52

STEP 35

(P.80 · 81)

■ Review of Step 34
(1) $y = 9 \times x$

(2) 1,350

1
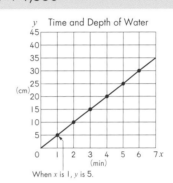
When x is 1, y is 5.

2
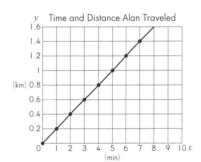

3 (1) $y = 150 \times x$

(2)
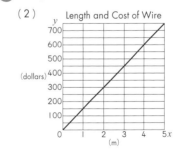

■ **Review of Step 35**

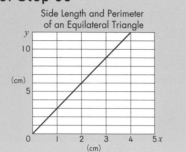

Side Length and Perimeter of an Equilateral Triangle

❶（1）30 　　　　　　（2）10

❷（1）1,000 m 　　　　（2）800 m
　（3）Anita 　　　　　（4）200 m

■ **Review of Step 36**
　（1）5 cm 　　　　　　（2）4 minutes

❶（1）

Time (min)	x	1	2	3	4	5	6	⋯
Volume (L)	y	2	4	6	8	10	12	⋯

×3

Ans. directly proportional

（2）

Length of rectangle (cm)	x	1	2	3	4	5	6	⋯
Width of rectangle (cm)	y	24	12	8	6	4.8	4	⋯

×3

Ans. inversely proportional

（3）

Length of rectangle (cm)	x	1	2	3	4	5	6	⋯
Width of rectangle (cm)	y	8	7	6	5	4	3	⋯

×3

Ans. neither

（4）

Height of parallelogram (cm)	x	1	2	3	4	5	6	⋯
Base of parallelogram (cm)	y	36	18	12	9	7.2	6	⋯

×3

Ans. inversely proportional

■ **Review of Step 37**
　（1）inversely proportional
　（2）directly proportional

❶（1）

Length (cm)	x	1	2	3	4	5	6	⋯
Width (cm)	y	24	12	8	6	4.8	4	⋯
$x \times y$		24	24	24	24	24	24	⋯

　（2）$x \times y = 24$ 　　$y = 24 \div x$

❷（1）$y = 12 \div x$
　（2）$y = 18 \div x$

❸（1）the distance of the trip
　（2）yes
　（3）$y = 120 \div x$
　（4）2.5

■ **Review of Step 38**
　2

❶（A）x multiplied by $\dfrac{1}{3}$ 　　y multiplied by 3
　（B）x multiplied by $\dfrac{1}{2}$ 　　y multiplied by 2

❷（1）（A）$\dfrac{1}{3}$ 　　（B）3
　（2）$y = 180 \div x$
　（3）$y = 180 \div 5 = 36$ 　　　　Ans. 36
　　　$y = 180 \div 15 = 12$ 　　　Ans. 12
　（4）$y = 180 \div x$ 　$1.8 = 180 \div x$
　　　$x = 180 \div 1.8 = 100$ 　　Ans. 100

■ Review of Step 39
(1) $y = 10 \div x$
(2) $y = 10 \div 4 = 2.5$　　　　Ans. 2.5

①
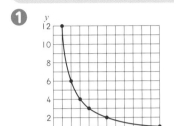

②
Length and Width for a Rectangle
with an Area of 24 Square Centimeters
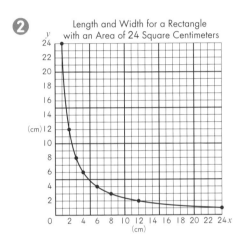

TEST (P.92 · 93)

Review of Step 32

Time (min)	x	1	2	3	4	5	6	7	⋯
Volume of water (L)	y	2	4	6	8	10	12	14	⋯

(2) It is also doubled.
(3) It is also multiplied by 4.
(4) yes

Review of Steps 33,34
$$y = 4 \times x$$

Review of Steps 35,36
(1) 450
(2) 4

Review of Step 37

Length (cm)	x	1	2	3	4	5	⋯
Width (cm)	y	18	9	6	4.5	3.6	⋯

(2) It is halved.
(3) It is multiplied by 4.
(4) yes

Review of Steps 38-40
(1) the distance of the trip
(2) $y = 840 \div x$
(3) 28

STEP 41 (P.94 · 95)

■ Review of Step 40
When x is 2⋯3　　　When y is 1⋯6

① (1) 1, 7　　2, 7
(2) $(8 + 6 + 5 + 9) \div 4 = 7$

② (1) $241 + 244 + 246 + 249 = 980$
Ans. 980 g
(2) $980 \div 4 = 245$　　　Ans. 245 g

③ $(55 + 56 + 54 + 55 + 58 + 53 + 54) \div 7 = 55$
Ans. 55 g

④ $(450 + 400 + 420 + 445 + 435) \div 5 = 430$
Ans. 430 g

STEP 42 (P.96 · 97)

■ Review of Step 41
84 g

① $(2 + 1 + 3 + 0 + 2) \div 5 = 1.6$
Ans. 1.6 students

② (1) $3 \times 20 = 60$　　　Ans. 60 km
(2) $0.7 \times 20 = 14$　　　Ans. 14 absences
(3) $0.6 \times 580 = 348$　　　Ans. 350 m
(4) $(6 + 5 + 7 + 0 + 8) \div 5 \times 20 = 104$
Ans. 104 books

■ Review of Step 42
$(257 + 261 + 259 + 263) \div 4 \times 20 = 5,200$
$5,200$ g $= 5.2$ kg   Ans. 5.2 kg

① $(265 \times 14 + 268 \times 16) \div 30 = 266.6$
                   Ans. 267 cm

② (1) $75 \times 3 = 225$ Ans. 225 points
   (2) $225 + 95 = 320$ Ans. 320 points
   (3) $320 \div 4 = 80$ Ans. 80 points

③ (1) $88 \times 4 = 352$ Ans. 352 points
   (2) $90 \times 5 = 450$ Ans. 450 points
   (3) $450 - 352 = 98$ Ans. 98 points

■ Review of Step 43
$(138.5 \times 4 + 135.5) \div 5 = 137.9$
                   Ans. 137.9 cm

① (1) $(48 + 53 + 63 + 58 + 65 + 53 + 58 + 56 + 57 + 58 + 55 + 60 + 50 + 67 + 57 + 62) \div 16 = 57.5$ Ans. 57.5 g
   (2) $(63 + 50 + 74 + 54 + 45 + 63 + 67 + 54 + 47 + 60 + 52 + 57 + 68) \div 13 = 58$ Ans. 58 g

② (1)

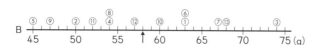

   (2) Chicken A   19 g   Chicken B   29 g
   (3) (as shown above)
   (4) the eggs from chicken B

■ Review of Step 44
Field 1   54 g   Field 2   96 g

①
(1)

Chicken A's Eggs (g)		Chicken B's Eggs (g)	
Mass range (g)	Number of eggs	Mass range (g)	Number of eggs
45 to 49.99	1	45 to 49.99	2
50 to 54.99	3	50 to 54.99	4
55 to 59.99	7	55 to 59.99	1
60 to 64.99	3	60 to 64.99	3
65 to 69.99	2	65 to 69.99	2
70 to 74.99	0	70 to 74.99	1
Total	16	Total	13

(2) A   1   B   2
(3) A $(2 + 0) \div 16 = 0.125$
                     Ans. about 13 %

     B $(2 + 1) \div 13 = 0.230...$
                     Ans. about 23 %

(4) 55 to 59.99 g

■ Review of Step 45
$(1 + 3) \div 13 = 0.30\overset{1}{7}$ Ans. 31 %

① (1) the range from 40 to 45 meters
   (2) 5 trees
   (3) $(3 + 1) \div 25 = 4 \div 25 = 0.16$
                   Ans. 16 %

② (1) team 2   (2) team 2

■ Review of Step 46
26 students

① (1) about 20 m
   (2) (as shown on the next page)
   (3) 25 to 29.99 m
       $6 \div 23 = 0.260...$ Ans. about 26 %

(2)

Distance range (m)	Students
5 to 9.99	2
10 to 14.99	5
15 to 19.99	4
20 to 24.99	5
25 to 29.99	6
30 to 34.99	1
Total	23

(4)

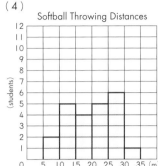

Softball Throwing Distances

STEP 48

(P.108・109)

■ Review of Step 47

(1) yes　　　(2) no　　　(3) yes

❶　123, 132, 213, 231, 312, 321

❷

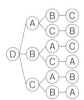

❸

Ans. 24 ways

STEP 49

(P.110・111)

■ Review of Step 48

6 ways

❶

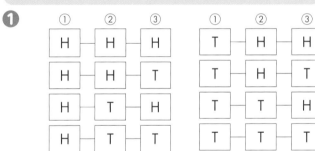

❷　(1) 0.1, 0.2, 0.3

(2) 0.1, 0.2, 0.3, 1.2, 1.3, 2.1, 2.3

❸　(1) $\frac{3}{4}$, $\frac{3}{5}$, $\frac{4}{5}$, $\frac{3}{6}$, $\frac{4}{6}$, $\frac{5}{6}$

(2) $\frac{4}{3}$, $\frac{5}{3}$, $\frac{6}{3}$, $\frac{5}{4}$, $\frac{6}{4}$, $\frac{6}{5}$

STEP 50

(P.112・113)

■ Review of Step 49

A-B, A-C, A-D, B-A, B-C, B-D, C-A,
C-B, C-D, D-A, D-B, D-C

❶

①	②	③		①	②	③
H	H	H		T	H	H
H	H	T		T	H	T
H	T	H		T	T	H
H	T	T		T	T	T

❷　(1) R-R, R-P, R-S, P-R, P-P, P-S, S-R,
S-P, S-S

(2) 3 ways

❸　1-6, 2-5, 3-4, 4-3, 5-2, 6-1

Ans. 6 ways

❹　A-B-C-F-I, A-B-E-F-I, A-B-E-H-I,
A-D-E-F-I, A-D-E-H-I, A-D-G-H-I

Ans. 6 routes

STEP 51 (P.114 · 115)

■ Review of Step 50
8 combinations

❶ A-B, A-C, A-D,
B-C, B-D,
C-D   Ans. 6 games

❷ A-B, A-C, A-D, A-E,
B-C, B-D, B-E,
C-D, C-E,
D-E   Ans. 10 games

❸ A-B, A-C, A-D, A-E, A-F,
B-C, B-D, B-E, B-F,
C-D, C-E, C-F,
D-E, D-F,
E-F   Ans. 15 matches

STEP 52 (P.116 · 117)

■ Review of Step 51
6 games

❶ (A, B, C) (B, C, D) (C, D, E)
(A, B, D) (B, C, E)
(A, B, E) (B, D, E)
(A, C, D)
(A, C, E)
(A, D, E)   Ans. 10 combinations

❷ (1) (A, B) (B, C) (C, D)
(A, C) (B, D)
(A, D)
(2) 6 combinations

❸ (1) (A, B, C) (B, C, D)
(A, B, D)
(A, C, D)
(2) 4 combinations

STEP 53 (P.118 · 119)

■ Review of Step 52
6 combinations

❶ 60 g, 110 g, 510 g, 150 g, 550 g,
600 g

❷ 6 g, 11 g, 15 g, 51 g, 55 g, 60 g

❸ 16 g, 56 g, 61 g, 65 g

❹ 100 g, 200 g, 500 g, 600 g, 700 g,
1,000 g, 1,100 g, 1,200 g

TEST (P.120 · 121)

Review of Steps 41-45
garden A

Review of Steps 46, 47
(1) 13 plums
(2) $3 \div 13 = 0.230...$ Ans. about 23 %

Review of Step 48
24 variations

Review of Step 49
12 numbers

Review of Step 50
8 outcomes

Review of Step 51
10 games

Review of Steps 52, 53
1 g, 2 g, 3 g, 4 g, 5 g, 6 g, 7 g

Ratios and Proportions Challenge (P.122 · 123)

Answers and sample solutions are provided below.
Solutions may vary.

1   (24 liters − 19 liters) ÷ 45 kilometers =
$\frac{1}{9}$ liter per kilometer
($\frac{1}{9}$ liter per km × 180 kilometers) +
24 liters = 44 liters

Ans. 44 L

⟨Tip⟩
As a first step, find the amount of gasoline that
the car uses to drive 1 kilometer.

2 (1) 72 − 42 = 30   Ans. 30 %
   (2) 91 − 72 = 19   40 × 0.19 = 7.6

Ans. 7.6 g

3   1,000 × 3.9 ÷ 1.5 = 2,600

Ans. 2,600 sheets

4   12 × 21 = 252 x × 28 = 252
252 ÷ 28 = 9   Ans. 9

5   36 odd numbers

⟨Tip⟩
In this case, for the number to be an odd
number, the ones place must be 1 or 3.
Zero cannot be used for the ten thousands
place.
If you write down all the possible numbers,
there are 6 odd numbers when the ten
thousands place is 1, and also 6 when it is 3.
There are 12 odd numbers when the ten
thousands place is 2, and also 12 when it is 4.
So, there are 36 odd numbers in total.

6   between 59th and 67th

⟨Tip⟩
First, consider the number of students who are
shorter than Emma.
The range that Emma is in is 150 cm to
154.99 cm, so sum up the students who are
shorter than this.
A: 2 + 4 + 7 + 11 + 7 = 31 students
B: 3 + 7 + 9 + 8 = 27 students
31 + 27 = 58 students
Next, consider the outcomes if Emma is either
the shortest or the tallest in her range. There
are 9 students in her range.
Emma is the shortest: $58 + 1 = 59^{th}$
Emma is the tallest: $58 + 9 = 67^{th}$

7   Brad and Alex's mean score: 160 ÷ 2 = 80
Number of points by which Brad and Alex's
mean score is lower than that of the other
3 people: 10 ÷ 2 = 5
The mean score of the other 3 people:
80 + 5 = 85
The mean score of all 5:
(80 + 80 + 85 + 85 + 85) ÷ 5 = 83

Ans. 83 points

⟨Tip⟩
Alex and Brad have scores that bring the
5-person group's total down by 10 points
(2 points times 5 people), compared to what
it would be if Alex and Brad had scored the
same as everyone else. Together, Alex and
Brad bring the total score down by 10,
so they each contribute 5 fewer points on
average than the other 3 people. Since Brad
and Alex's mean score is 80, the other
3 people must have a mean score of 85.
You can calculate the mean for all 5 of them
using this information.